THE SONNETS OF GIOVANNI PICO DELLA MIRANDOLA

A DUAL LANGUAGE TRANSLATION

Marc A Cirigliano

Copyright © 2024 Marc A Cirigliano

The moral right of the author has been asserted.

Apart from any fair dealing for the purposes of research or private study, or criticism or review, as permitted under the Copyright, Designs and Patents Act 1988, this publication may only be reproduced, stored or transmitted, in any form or by any means, with the prior permission in writing of the publishers, or in the case of reprographic reproduction in accordance with the terms of licences issued by the Copyright Licensing Agency. Enquiries concerning reproduction outside those terms should be sent to the publishers.

Troubador Publishing Ltd
Unit E2 Airfield Business Park,
Harrison Road, Market Harborough,
Leicestershire LE16 7UL
Tel: 0116 279 2299
Email: books@troubador.co.uk
Web: www.troubador.co.uk/matador

ISBN 978-1-80514-520-2

British Library Cataloguing in Publication Data.
A catalogue record for this book is available from the British Library.

Typeset in 11pt Minoin Pro by Troubador Publishing Ltd, Leicester, UK

for annamaria and giancarlo moneti

Contents

Acknowledgements	vii
Beautiful, Clever, Enticing Little Words	1
On the vernacular in late quattrocento Florence	1
The duecento and trecento background on the vernacular	3
Pico on Dante and Petrarch	9
Pico's remaking of the status quo	11
Pico's poetic style	14
Critical judgements of Pico's sonnets	20
Reading Pico's sonnets	22
A note on the translations	27
Bibliography	30
THE SONNETS	33
Notes on Pico's sonnets	81
Endnotes	115

Acknowledgements

A good many people helped, in one way or another, in the process of completing this translation.

Nicola Allain was kind in her support, as were my colleagues in the Arts and Media Department, in my receiving a sabbatical to finish this project. Alan Pascuzzi encouraged the project from inception to completion. Dan Mariotti checked on me regularly to see if I was keeping apace. Paola Vallatta offered some suggestions with some translations. Lesia Vincent and Suzanne Erickson each were generous with their time and thoughts in offering suggestions on the manuscript as it reached final form. George Ferzoco and Jeremy Thompson were extremely patient waiting and waiting for the manuscript. Above all, my lovely wife Lindy helped me all along the way.

Beautiful, Clever, Enticing Little Words

Marc A. Cirigliano

ON THE VERNACULAR IN LATE QUATTROCENTO FLORENCE

The major medium that expanded the possibilities for change and innovation in Quattrocento Florence was the defiant insistence on using the vernacular as an equal but infinitely more accessible means of communication than Latin. Although initially advocated by Dante's teacher Brunetto Latini and then championed successively in the Trecento by Dante Alighieri and then Francesco Petrarca, the Tuscan vernacular still needed intellectual advocacy well into the Quattrocento. The political and cultural might of the Holy See as a bastion of established political and religious power insisted on Latin as the official and naturally superior language. There was to be none of this vernacular stuff.

As Derrida clarifies:

> The fact that access to the written sign assures the sacred power of keeping existence operative within the trace and of knowing the general structure of the universe; that all clergies, exercising political power or not, were constituted at the same time as writing and by the disposition of graphic power ... remains indestructible...[1]

Championing the vernacular, Florence, under the patronage of Piero de' Cosimo (1416-1469), held a vernacular poetry contest, the *Certame coronario*, in the *Duomo* on October 22, 1441. An emulation of poetry contests from Antiquity, the theme was *La vera amicizia* (True Friendship), with no contestant winning, but poets producing genuine variety and serious attempts at emulating classical meter.[2]

If the vernacular was to be considered the language of the learned on par with Latin, we might see an analogous contemporary development with the art of painting. Leon Battista Alberti wrote—of his collegial pictorial innovators Donatello, Masaccio, Ghiberti, Luca della Robbia and Brunelleschi—in his treatise on painting *Della pittura*, "We, however, delight in having taken the palm in daring to recommend this very subtle and noble art to letters."[3]

A full generation later in 1476, Lorenzo de' Medici (1449-1492) would speak of the origin and quality of the Tuscan vernacular poets in a letter to the curious young prince Federico d'Aragona, later to be King of Naples (1451-1504, King 1496-1504):

> Nor, for that reason, is there anyone who despises this Tuscan language as less ornamented and less copious. Because, if its riches and ornaments will be well and rightly appreciated, this language will be considered neither poor nor rough, but abundant and most polished.

Lorenzo clarifies the qualities of Tuscan, the vernacular:

> Anything gentle, florid, graceful, ornate—anything acute, distinct, ingenious, subtle—anything large and copious, anything tall, magnificent, sonorous—and finally, any other ardent, spirited, excited thing can be imagined.[4]

Lorenzo went so far as to create with Angelo Poliziano an anthology for Federico of 200 poems from the Duecento on, including his own. Since lost, the so-called *Raccolta aragonese*, circulated among the courts of Italy, with a copy lent to Isabella d'Este in 1512, was influential, elevating Tuscan as the language of poetry and subsequently cementing it as the language of Italy.[5]

Lorenzo further explains the importance of the Tuscan vernacular and the leading Florentine poets in his *Comment on His Own Sonnets*:

> And yet, wanting to prove the dignity of our language, we only have to insist on the first conditions: if our language easily expresses any concept of our mind; and to this no better reason can be introduced than experience. Dante, Petrarch and Boccaccio, our Florentine poets, have in their serious and very sweet verses and orations shown very clearly that it is very easy to be able to express every sense in this language.

He gets more specific on the respective strengths of each poet, beginning with Dante:

Because whoever reads Dante's *Comedy* will find many theological and natural things expressed with great dexterity and ease. He will still find in his most apt writing those three generations of styles which are praised by the orators; that is, humble, mediocre and high. Then, in effect, in only one, Dante has the most perfectly absolute in what is found in various authors, both Greek and Latin … Dante's *canzoni* and sonnets are of such gravity, subtlety and ornamentation that they have almost no comparison in prose and solid oration.

Lorenzo goes on to specifics on Petrarch:

Who will deny that in Petrarch there is a serious, lepid, and gentle style—and these amorous things are treated with such gravity and loveliness, undoubtedly not found in Ovid, Tibullus, Catullus, Propertius or any other Latin?

He then describes Boccaccio's verse with great praise:

Anyone who has read Boccaccio, a very learned and creative man, will easily judge singular and unique in the world not only for his invention, but also his copiousness and eloquence.[6]

THE DUECENTO AND TRECENTO BACKGROUND ON THE VERNACULAR

It was Dante's teacher Brunetto Latini (c.1225-1294) who emphasized what would become the central ideas of Tuscan vernacular poetry when he wrote in his *Il Tesoretto* (lines 398-426) that poetry (and prose) should be economical, clear, didactic, harmonious, unified and, in order to be understood, composed in the spoken, common language of the people "so you understand and learn."[7]

In fact, with his ground-breaking *Vita nova* (1292-94) Dante championed the vernacular with a sequence of poems interspersed with prose analyses of his form, content and intentions. Slightly later in his *De vulgari eloquentia* (1302-05), a Latin treatise on the eloquence of the vernacular, Dante begins, "I shall try, inspired by the Word that comes from above, to say something useful about the language of people who speak the vulgar tongue." He then goes on to clarify:

I call "vernacular language" that which infants acquire from those around them when they first begin to distinguish sounds; or, to put it more succinctly, I declare that vernacular language is that which we learn without any formal instruction, by imitating our nurses.

Dante draws a distinction between the *vernacular* and what he labels as the more formal *grammar*:

There also exists another kind of language, at one remove from us, which the Romans called *gramatica* [grammar]. The Greeks and some - but not all - other peoples also have this secondary kind of language. Few, however, achieve complete fluency in it, since knowledge of its rules and theory can only be developed through dedication to a lengthy course of study.

We arrive at the central point of Dante, that the vernacular is the more noble of the two:

Of these two kinds of language, the more noble is the vernacular: first, because it was the language originally used by the human race; second, because the whole world employs it, though with different pronunciations and using different words; and third, because it is natural to us, while the other is, in contrast, artificial. And this more noble kind of language is what I intend to discuss.

Interesting to see these three reasons in support of the vernacular: 1) The language originally used by humans; 2) The whole world uses it; and, 3) "It is natural to us," not artificial.[8]

Yet, there is more to it as Dante, speaking specifically of poetry, explains his approach in one of his *canzoni*:

Così nel mio parlar voglio esser aspro
com'è ne li atti questa bella petra ...

I want to be as rare and biting in my poetry
as this beautiful stone is in her actions ...

Dante distinguishes that he wants to be as *aspro*, meaning *harsh*, in his *parlar*, his *poetry*, as that *bella petra*, that *beautiful stone*, a metaphor for his *hard* lady, is in her actions. This is a sharp break from the *Dolce stil nuovo* (Sweet New Style), whose recent heritage comes from both the Sicilian school and the troubadours in Provence, that deals with matters that are *sweet* with ladies who are both *gentle* and *graceful*. Dante goes beyond this heritage. He expands the subject matter of love poetry so that it embraces the reality of the human love experience, both its elation, but also its unsuccessful and even tragic moments. Hence, we have the adjective *aspro*, a very loaded word that can be translated as *harsh, rough, sharp, fierce, acrid* and *shrill*. If we link that to the nature of his lady, a fine polished stone, then comes also the sense of *hard* and *rarity*, so that one way to translate this term is *biting and rare*, both describing his lady's actions and the manner of his poetry in expressing that *biting* sense.

To capture this brutal side of unrequited love, further in this *canzone*, Dante exclaims:

> *Ahi angosciosa e dispietata lima*
> *che sordamente la mia vita scemi …*
>
> Ah-h-h! anguishing and merciless mud
> that secretly rots my life …[9]

Consequently, when Dante's poetry is characterized as *rozza* (rough), it is not that he struggles with words as a poet, but rather, that he expresses suffering and anguish in his lyric poetry and aspects of damnation in the *Inferno* of his *Commedia*, where he speaks of *la gente perduta*, the lost people.

There is more.

At the beginning of his poetic *oeuvre*, Dante writes in prose in his *Vita nova*:

> When so many days had passed that nine years were exactly complete since the above-described apparition of this most gentle lady, on the last of these days it happened that this admirable lady appeared to me, clothed in purest white, between two gentle ladies who were of greater age; and, passing along a street, turned her eyes toward that place where I stood very timidly; and by her ineffable courtesy, which is to-day rewarded in the eternal world, saluted me with such virtue that it seemed to me then that I saw all the bounds of bliss.[10]

After Dante has a vision of *Amor* coming to bind him with his vision of Beatrice, he writes, "And thinking on what had appeared to me, I resolved to make it known to many who were famous poets at that time."[11]

As such, with Dante seeing Beatrice among other ladies in the streets of Florence, his willingness to share that experience with other poets, and, in his *Commedia*, his judgments of people with their interactions with others and society as a whole, it is easy to conclude that Dante's poetry is *social*.

Petrarch, in a very different turn, bases his poetry on reflection, meditation and solitude.[12] He begins his *Rerum vulgarium fragmenta*:

> *Voi ch' ascoltate in rime sparse il suono*
> *di quei sospiri ond' io nudriva 'l core*
> *in sul mio primo giovenile errore,*
> *quand' era in parte altr' uom da quel ch' i' sono,*
>
> *del vario stile in ch' io piango et ragiono*
> *fra le vane speranze e 'l van dolore…*
>
> O you who hear within these scattered verses
> the sound of sighs with which I fed my heart
> in my first errant youthful days when I
> in part was not the man I am today;
>
> for all the ways in which I weep and speak
> between vain hopes, between vain suffering…[13]

Petrarch, then, sets the stage for his poetic narration of his many years dealing with love. And, he begins to explain his unique position, in a sense, separate from, as the *other*, as he continues in his opening poem of a poetic sequence that consists of 366 poems.

> *Ma ben veggio or sì come al popol tutto*
> *favola fui gran tempo, onde sovente*
> *di me medesmo meco mi vergogno…*
>
> But now I see how I've become the talk
> so long a time of people all around,
> (it often makes me feel so full of shame) …[14]

Indeed, people talk of him while he has been on this journey as he struggles with love, composing poems about it. It is this isolation, then, that Petrarch emphasizes that he composed his entire epic poetic sequence.

> Solo et pensoso i più deserti campi
> vo mesurando a passi tardi et lenti,
> et gli occhi porto per fuggire intenti ove
> vestigio uman la rena stampi…
>
> Alone and deep in thought I measure out
> the most deserted fields, with slow, late steps,
> with eyes intent to flee whatever sign
> of human footprint left within the sand…[15]

In fact, in writing to his brother Gherardo in order to explain the meaning of a sequence of Latin *Eclogues* he sent to him in a letter, Petrarch says, "I always have felt, from my earliest childhood, a hatred of cities, implanted in me by nature, and a love of sylvan life…"[16] As Petrarch describes to his brother the two main characters of these pastoral poems, Sylvius and Monicus, he tells his brother, "For you have now a sure abode, and consequently a fairly sure hope of sepulture, while I am still wandering about at random, and everything in my future is quite unsure."[17]

But, Petrarch not only identifies himself as a man of solitude, a wanderer and a man *about whom people talk* because there is a social aspect to his poetry, for he, too, talks of others, of society when he writes:

> *Standomi un giorno solo a la fenestra*
> *onde cose vedea tante et si nove*
> *ch' era sol di mirar quasi già stanco,*
> *una fera m'apparve da man destra*
> *con fronte umana da far arder Giove,*
> *cacciata da duo veltri, un nero, un bianco,*
> *che l'un et l'altro flanco*
> *de la fera gentil mordean si forte*
> *che 'n poco tempo la menaro al passo*
> *ove chiusa in un sasso*
> *vinse molta bellezza acerba morte,*
> *et mi fe' sospirar sua dura sorte…*
>
> One day while at my window all alone,
> where I saw many and such strange things happen

merely looking at them made me weary,
I saw a beast appear on my right side
with human face to make Jove flare with love
pursued by two swift hounds, one black one white,
who dug their teeth so deep
into both sides of such a noble beast
that in no time they forced her to the pass
where, trapped within the stone,
untimely death then vanquished such great beauty,
and I sighed from the sight of her harsh fate…[18]

This poem goes on with five other examples of goodness destroyed in the world. Yet, the initial stanza is Petrarch's metaphor about the world destroying beauty, which is Petrarch's view of others in the world.

Standomi is not an isolated example. Such an attitude appears throughout the *Canzoniere*. For example, in *Spirto gentil che quelle membra reggi*, we have a criticism of Italy:

Che s'aspetti non so, né che s'agogni Italia,
che suoi guai non par che senta,
vecchia oziosa et lenta …

For what Italy waits or yearns I know not,
for she does not appear to feel her woes—
she's idle, slow, and old …[19]

And, in, *Italia mia, ben che 'l parlar sia indarno*, Petrarch reprises his criticism:

Italia mia, ben che 'l parlar sia indarno
a le piaghe mortali
che nel bel corpo tuo sì spesse veggio …

O, my own Italy, though words be useless
to heal the mortal wounds
I see covering all your lovely body …[20]

It is, then, Dante and Petrarch who were innovators with the vernacular, writing in different but intense ways about human relationships, and seeing society for what it was, often the worst, something Pico is intimately familiar with.

PICO ON DANTE AND PETRARCH

With Dante and Petrarch, as well as Lorenzo de' Medici's thoughts on both of them, in mind, we come to Pico's thoughts on poetry, both through a letter he wrote to Lorenzo de' Medici and, most importantly, his own sonnet sequence.[21]

We can glean significant insight into Pico's judgments on poetry from a letter he wrote to Lorenzo de' Medici in July of 1484. In the letter, a lengthy *encomium* of both Lorenzo and his poetry, Pico shares insights on both Dante and Petrarch.

Pico begins by praising Lorenzo as a poet mature beyond his years:

> I have read, Lorenzo de' Medici, your poems, which the vernacular Muses suggested to you during your tender age. I acknowledged the legitimate making of the Muses and Graces; I did not recognize the work of a tender age. For whom has not felt in your rhymes the numerous verses dancing to the Graces? Who does not hear the Muses singing in a melodious manner and tune?[22]

Pico then moves to Dante and Petrarch:

> There are among you two chiefly celebrated poets of the Florentine language, Francesco Petrarch and Dante Alighieri, of whom I have said that to the whole world, that they are of the learned. There are those who desire things in Francesco. Words in Dante. In you he who has a mind and ears, neither would be desirable, in which it is not possible to see whether things are more enlightened by speech, or words by sentences.[23]

What does Pico mean by *res* in Petrarch's poetry and *verba* in Dante's? *Res* in Latin, may mean *thing* or *things*, but, more broadly, in the sense of his title for his poetic sequence, *Rerum vulgarium fragmenta*, or, the Italian translation, *rime sparse*, we have *fragments of ordinary things*.[24] In this sense, then, *res* may mean *day to day affairs* or *matters of personal concern*. With Dante, *verba*, the plural accusative of *verbum*, meaning *word*, deals with the breadth of Dante's *Commedia* expressed in *words*. Hence, *verba* denotes a wide ranging vocabulary, greater than Petrarch's, in which Dante poeticizes the vastness of the human social experience. We must use *social* here, because so much of Dante deals with what people do to each other.

Pico then talks of Petrarch's characteristics:

> ... Francesco revives what concerns the senses ... But to me his sweetness is, so to speak, sweetly sour and sweetly austere. He was eloquent and equable ... he is tender and soft ... He is voluptuous and melodious ...[25]

Yet, Pico does see limitations in Petrarch's verse, "Francesco, who has something to entice in the first instance, but does not satisfy further..."[26]

This is a judgement worthy of consideration. The last statement that Petrarch *does not satisfy further* reminds us of Matthew Arnold on Percy Bysshe Shelly as a "beautiful and ineffectual angel, beating in the void his luminous wings in vain." Although an unfair exaggeration in its broad dismissal of Shelley, Arnold's point is somewhat analogous to what Pico says of Petrarch, when we are in the middle of the *Canzoniere* and we feel like shouting, "Get on with it, man!"

Pico also gets to a central point on Dante:

> Certainly, as far as style is concerned, I think no one will deny you that Dante is sometimes hideous, rough, and lean, so that he is much crude and impure, even his goldsmiths admit this.[27]

Yet, Dante's subject matter embraces the entire human experience, much of which is filled with deceit, deception, and, at its worst, violence—each of which makes ample "hideous, rough and lean" subject matter for parts of his *Commedia*.

Pico criticizes Dante's shortcoming on one of the central thems in the *Commedia*:

> If it is about God, about the soul, about the blessed, Thomas brings what Augustine wrote about these things, and he was as frequent as he was constant in discussing and meditating on these things, you in carrying out the most important public and private business. It was not so clear in Dante that he had done this, as that he had not done it.[28]

George Steiner makes a strong point when he hypothesizes that society should jettison criticism and experience works of art, theater, movies, music and literature deeply on their own, memorizing the works, experience them deeply "in the most direct ways possible." In this society, critics do not tell people what to think and how to react to creative works. As Steiner explains, "Interpretation is, to the largest possible degree, lived."

This is because, "All serious art, music and literature is a critical act." Serious creation is both a "criticism of life" and, as well, "an expository reflection on, a value judgement of, the inheritance and context to which they pertain."[29]

Pico had a prodigious memory. He knew Dante's *Commedia* so well that he could recite it backwards. No doubt he had a penetrating knowledge of Dante's lyric poetry, Petrarch *Rerum vulgarium fragmenta*, and Boccaccio's verse.

With this in mind, coupled with Steiner's suggested reading and not simply analyzing literature, it is easy to conclude that when Pico wrote his own sonnets, he was commenting on his Tuscan forebears and going beyond what his poetic ancestors had done. His was no mere hero worship of emulation. This is borne out, too, in his own criticism when he discussed Dante, Petrarch and Boccaccio with Lorenzo. He created his own poetry or formulated his own critical judgments as an equal.

Other Italians may see these three poets from the point of view of being fans, but not Pico, whose poetry should not be seen in simple comparison to that of his predecessors, but as poetry in its own right, read for its independent self, not for whom it might resemble. Or, as Steiner suggests, as "an expository reflection on, a value judgement of, the inheritance … "

PICO'S REMAKING OF THE STATUS QUO

Although Pico lived a privileged life, as did many aristocrats of his time, he did so very much on his own terms. By that, he was talented, forthright and original. He was unique. Savonarola saw to it that the inscription on his tomb read:

Joannes jacet hic Mirandola: cætera norunt
Et Tagus, et Ganges, forsan et Antipodes.

Giovanni Pico lies here: the others know
And the Tagus, and the Ganges, and perhaps the Antipodes.

Indeed, he was known from Spain to India—and, perhaps, to the other side of the world.

Although Pico grew into one of the finest minds of his contemporary Italy, he did come from impressive roots. Giovanni Pico della Mirandola (February 24, 1463) was born near Modena in Mirandola, an independent aristocratic county which was coupled with the county of Concordia. He was the youngest of five children of Gianfrancesco I Pico, Lord of Mirandola and Count of Concordia, and his wife Giulia, daughter of Feltrino Boiardo, Count of Scandiano. The family was well-heeled. Pico's mother was cousin to the noted writer and poet Matteo Maria Boiardo, famous for his epic poem *Orlando innamorato*.

From the time his mother took him to Bologna in the summer of 1473 so Cardinal Francesco Gonzaga might declare him a papal protonotary *at the age of ten*, we see a prodigious mind continually develop between the sophisticated urban centers of Bologna, Pavia, Ferrara, Padova and Florence as he meets such philosophers, theologians and intellectuals as Marsilio Ficino, Lorenzo il Magnifico, Angelo Poliziano, Egidio da Viterbo, Girolamo Benivieni, Girolamo Balbi, Yohanan Alemanno, Elia del Medigo and Girolamo Savonarola.

Socially, he did what he wanted. He characterized himself broadly, "Of course, while I am twins, as they say, wanting to sit alone and be at last, as I will say in a few words, neither poet, nor orator, nor philosopher."[30] Pico was intellectually deep and, at the same time, versatile. He did strike out on his own, crafting radical new viewpoints. The essence of his being was that of innovator, non-conformist, genius.

He reconciled Plato and Aristotle, putting Plato under Aristotle, in his *De ente et uno* (On Being and the One). With his syncretic *900 Theses*, the first book to be banned by the Church, he challenged anyone to debate him in St. Peter's in Rome on the shared principles of the world's major religions. He delved deeply into the Hebrew-based Kabbalah and hermeticism, seeking an alternative path to salvation and truth outside the Christian tradition. Later he would attack astrology, much to the chagrin of his mentor Marsilio Ficino, with his *Disputationes adversus astrologiam divinicatrium* (Disputations against the Astrology of the Divines).[31]

If it were not enough to rile the philosophers, theologians and astrologers— and, as we have seen, diminish the poetry of both Dante and Petrarch—somewhere within this, he would manage, while in Arezzo, to have an affair with Margherita, the wife of Giuliano Mariotto de' Medici, one of Lorenzo de' Medici's cousins. On or around May 10, 1486, was a scandal, no doubt, as he tried to run off with Margherita under the protection of his own armed militia. Interdicted in nearby Bastardo by husband Giuliano's own soldiers, well over a dozen of Pico's men were killed, him wounded twice and severely beaten, with Margherita returned.[32] Pico, traumatized, was imprisoned, saved only when Lorenzo de' Medici intervened for his eventual release.

Was he a changed man after this?

A letter by sister-in-law Costanza says that after his amorous debacle, Pico "gave himself to extraordinary penance." In addition, in a letter from October 15, 1486, Pico wrote from Perugia to Andrea Corneo d'Urbino:

> It is not that you miss my Etruscan poems; after all, a long time ago we left my message of amorous filth, thinking of other things.

Further, we also know that he visited the *bonfire of the vanities* in Florence, as Sir Thomas More translates:

> Five books that in his youth of wanton verses of love with other like fantasies he had made in his vulgar tongue: all together (in detestation of his vice passed) and lest these trifles might be some evil occasion afterward, he burned them.[33]

Was Pico's contrition genuine or expedient? As Brian P. Copenhaver clarifies:

> It may be that the disasters of 1486–7 chastened the young nobleman enough to explain the muffling of Kabbalah in the *Heptaplus* and the jarring recantation that we find in the *Disputations*. But since the editor of the *Disputations*, Gianfrancesco Pico, also edited the letters that he selected to underwrite a tendentious *Life* of his uncle, and since Gianfrancesco himself was not just a devout fideist but also a prodigiously productive scholar and an original thinker, we should not dismiss the possibility that the *Disputations* ought to be read more as a pendant to the nephew's *Life* of Pico than as proof of penitence in a final phase of his uncle's meteoric career.[34]

Indeed, Pico's personal redemption may have been more his nephew's attempt at miliorating his late uncle's reputation in the eyes of the Church and history.

In sum, looking at Pico *in toto*, might depend on one's viewpoint. To modern eyes, delving into various religious traditions as part of a spiritual quest, rejecting an established irrationality such as astrology, engaging in creative writing through poetry and having an intense affair with a married woman might seem completely modern. What's the big deal, we might ask today? Well, to the eyes of those in power in late Quattrocento Italy, the big deals were each of those actions. For us today, this might be a propitious beginning for a relatively young man. For them back then, it rattled the Great Chain of Being. So much so, that it led to Pico's end. Recent forensic evidence has shown that Pico, along with a friend, poet Angelo Poliziano, were poisoned. Pico died in Florence on November 17, 1494 at the age of 31, the victim of assassination, with modern science assuring us that he was poisoned with arsenic.[35]

PICO'S POETIC STYLE

Using his contemporary vernacular creatively, Pico wrote sonnets with his own unique blend of Tuscan and some Latin vocabulary synthesized into his own poetic voice. He was conventional in using the established sonnet form, while original in developing his own poems. Pico may have used the same fourteen line sonnet that so many others did, but his own voice was creatively imbued with aspects of the Latin period and such rhetorical devices as *apocopation*, *hyperbaton*, *ellipsis* and *anaphora* that his poetry demands a close analysis.

Following the poetic convention of his time, he uses the standard hendecasyllable (*endecasillabo*) line, a line of eleven syllables that emulates classical Latin amd Greek poetry. This line has two minor accents on the second and sixth syllable and a major accent on the tenth syllable. We can see an example of this in the first line of Dante's *Commedia*:

Nel **me**zzo del ca**mm**in di nostra **vi**ta ...

Or, the first line of Petrarch's *RVF*:

Voi **ch'as**coltate in **ri**me sparse il **suo**no ...

Common in Italian poetry from the Duecento into modern times, a dipthong, two vowels together, such as the *uo* in *suono* counts as one syllable, known as *syneresis*. Grammatically they count as two, but poetically, they count as one syllable. However, sometimes poets use a *dieresis* over the first vowel of a dipthong, a mark that looks like a German *umlaut*, to make each letter count as a syllable in order to make the line have eleven syllables and not ten.[36]

Here we have two examples of the same word, the first with a dieresis and the second with syneresis:

voi, gentil crïatura - Frederick II
Cusì, gentil criatura - Guido delle Colonne

Sequential vowels are not simply counted as one syllable or two within a word, but also through the linking of vowels in sequential words or their separation, known respectively as a *synaleph* and a *dialeph*.

Here we an example of dialeph followed by synaleph:

> *senza in cui si mise* – Giacomo da Lentini
> *Chiare, fresche et dolci acque* - Petrarch

In Lentini's example, there is a break between *senza* and *in*, so they count as two poetic syllables. In Petrarch's line, *fresche* blends with *et*, so there are two syllables here and not three. *Dolci* blends with *acque* to make three syllables instead of four.

Pico uses the dieresis as needed.

In Sonnet 14:10, Pico places a dieresis over the *u* to denote that the dipthong *süo* counts as two syllables, not the usual one.

> *che, mal per me, fui süo, se l'antica*
> which, bad for me, I was his, thus his

In Sonnet 21:1, Pico uses a dieresis mark over the *I* in *Io*, *Ïo* in order to make this dipthong count as two syllables, not as the normal one syllable, so that the line has the usual eleven syllables.

> *Ïo temo che a lingua non consenta*
> *el cor ...*
> I fear that my heart does not agree with
> my words ...

In Sonnet 33:4, we have:

> *chi furar volse la febëa lampa.*
> to whoever wanted to steal the Phoeban lamp.

Normally, the *ea* in *febea* would be counted as one syllable, but with the dieresis on the *e*, *febëa*, Pico adds an extra syllable of the word to fit the hendecasyllabic line. *Febea* is another term for *Apollonian*, where *Phoebus* is another name for *Apollo*.

Pico also uses another practice of his contemporary poetry, apocopation (*apocope*), the cutting off of a word ending. Some of his most frequent are changing

Amore to *Amor*, while *cielo* becomes *ciel* or even *cel*. Other examples include *cantare* becoming *cantar*, *loro* changes to *lor*, or *fuori* simply becomes *for*, and *cuore* reduces to *cor*. Apocopation can lower the syllable count to fit a given idea into the 11 syllable line, simplifies the pronunciation so that the line reads *out loud* more quickly thereby intensifying the expression, or transforms the line into something closer to the actual spoken word. If *cuore* becomes *cor*, it can make for a closer bond between poet and an audience that only speaks *il volgare*.

Another device that Pico uses is *hyperbaton*, a not normal word order. This requires some explanation.

Word order in Italian in general, and in Italian poetry in particular, is different than it is in English. The word order in Latin is also very different than English. We write English in loose sentences, with a word's meaning determined by word order within a sentence. But in Italian and Latin, it can be common, for emphasis, to put the subject at the very end, a practice you cannot do in English loose sentences. For instance, in English you might say, "I want to read that book this evening." This translates into Italian, "*Io voglio legere questo libro stasera*." Yet, in Italian, the subject pronoun *io* can be omitted, as in, "*Voglio legere …*," or placed at the end for emphasis, "*Voglio legere questo libro stasera io*," as in, "I really want to read …"

An example of a hyperbaton in Latin would be:

Instabilis in istum plurimum *fortuna* valuit : *omnes* invidiose eripuit bene vivendi casus *facultates* …
Unstable Fortune has exercised her greatest power on this creature. All the means of living well Chance has jealously taken from him … [37]

In a normal loose sentence, *fortuna* would come immediately after *instabilis*, as we see in the translation. And, in the next phrase, *facultates* would be moved forward to right after *omnes*. However, here the great Roman writer Cicero emphasizes both *instability* and *Fortune* in the first phrase and who they affect in the next with this hyperbaton.

Pico jumbles his word order in his sonnets. He infuses his poetic Tuscan and Latin with *hyperbaton*, often doing so either to meet the existing rhyme scheme of a sonnet or create a poetic emphasis—or, both.

In Sonnet 2:6, when Pico writes, *che invidia move Apollo* (so to move Apollo to envy), we again have a Latinate construction that would be, in a loose sentence in modern Italian, *che muove Apollo ad invidia*. Pico's hyperbatonic phrasing here both fits the rhyme scheme and places emphasis that *Apollo* is moved by her.

Again in Sonnet 2, in the final terzina, Pico separates subject from verb and direct object to amplify his narrative more completely. The terzina reads:

*Le belle acorte **parolette** vaghe*
nel cor se l'anidaro, che poi spesso
*per volar d'indi indarno **spiega l'ale**.*

The beautiful, clever, enticing **little words**,
if they nested in the heart, often then **explain**,
in order—in vain—to fly from there, **the wings**.

Further here, Pico uses the Florentine third person form of the verb *spiegare* to stand for the third person plural.

Another example of of a Latinate construction is Pico's use of *hyperbaton* is in Sonnet 30:11, *però parte nel ciel non avrai meco* that would read in modern Italian as *però non avrai parte con me nel ciel*. *Meco* is from the Latin *mecum* (with me). With what is a jumbled word order to us, while thinking, in part, in Latin, Pico has created a phrasing that both fits the rhyme scheme while emphasizing that he does not want his spirit with him. The *terzina* reads:

Sordido sei e maculato e cieco,
e più mi sdegno essendo tu nostra opra:
***però parte nel ciel non avrai meco**.*

You're dirty and spotted and blind,
and I'm more sorry you're our creation:
however, part in heaven, you will not have with me.

Pico also used *ellipsis*, the practice, the conventional omission of a word or words in a phrase or sentence which occurs in all languages. In English, we might say, "Dante writes poetry. Petrarch, too," when the meaning is, "Dante writes poetry. Petrarch *writes poetry*, too." Or, the common expression *How are you doing?* has simplified to *What's up?* or simply *Sup?* a clever contraction of the former where ellipsis reigns and one new slang word implies or connotes all the others in that old traditional greeting.

Continuing on, instead of saying *io voglio*, you can say *voglio*. This becomes more complicated in Pico's poetry because ellipsis is common in Latin. For example, the

Latin phrase *Pax vobiscum*, literally means *Peace with you*, but the sense is better rendered in *[May] peace [be] with you*. In Pico, we have in Sonnet 10:5, *Tanto può in me*, which means *Tanto può **essere** (or **stare**) in me*. Or, in Sonnet 18:8, *qual la sua fiamma*, which is ellipitcal for *quale è la sua fiamma*.

Sometimes, Pico combines ellipsis and hyperbaton. In Sonnet 28:4, when Pico writes *che empieti de triunfi soi le carte*, the normal word order would read *che empiti i suoi trionfi delle carte*. In this hyperbaton, we also have an ellipsis where the phrase would read *which completed his triumphs* **[predicted by]** *the Tarot*.

We find one of the more difficult lines in Sonnet 14 4: *manco quel tracto fuor de l'unda pesce* is a hyperbaton and also an ellipsis. Literally, *I lack that trait outside of the wave fish*. The sense is: *manco quel tracto* **[come un]** *pesce fuori dell'unda*, which translated here as *I lack strength just like a fish out of the wave (or water)*.

In Sonnet 36:9, Pico's lady asks for pity from one who would not forgive and she would then discover his heart. *Ella a pietà non ch'a perdon si volse*, an elliptical hyerbaton that reads, literally, *She to pity not who would to pardon turn*. Poetically in English, the following might work, but sound antiquated: *She to pity who would not turn to pardon*. The meaning, though, is: *She asked for pity from who would not pardon*.

Pico also uses *anafora*, the repetition of a word or phrase for emphasis. In *Sonnet 5*, he begins twelve of the sonnet's fourteen lines with *Amor* or *Amore*. In the first quatrain:

> **Amor**, *focoso giacio e fredda face;*
> **Amor**, *mal dilectoso e dolce affanno;*
> **Amor**, *pena suave et util danno;*
> **Amor**, *eterna guerra senza pace.*

> **Love**, fiery ice and cold torch;
> **Love**, most loving illness and sweet breathlessness;
> **Love**, sweet pain and helpful wound;
> **Love**, eternal war without peace.

In *Sonnet 20*, we have an extended *anafora* where each phrase begins with *se* (if), creating a long compound dependent clause with the main clause in *line 11, el lamentar non vale*. The first quatrain reads:

> **Se** *non spenge el mio fuoco el fiume eterno*

ch'Amor versa da gli ochi, e il piancto molto
se 'l desir cresce, e lo sperar m'è tolto,
e tuttavia m'afflige el caldo interno …

If the eternal river does not quench my fire
that Love pours from the eyes and **if** my desire
grows my tears a lot and hope is taken from me,
and still my hot insides plague me …

In *Sonnet 38*, we read a seven line example of *anaphora*, using the preposition *per* repetitively at the beginning of each phrase, which builds intensity. In the first quatrain, we see:

Per *quel velo che porti agli ochi avinto*
*e **per** colei che si creò ne l'acque,*
pel *bel paese ove la Ninfa nacque*
per cui fusti da te legato e vinto …

For that blindfold that you wear bound to the eyes
and **for** she who was created in the waters,
for the beautiful country where the Nymph was born,
for whom you were bound and defeated …

Pico also uses the Latin period in the creation of his quatrains, terzinas and even an entire sonnet as a whole. In Sonnet 1:5, *lei* (she) is mentioned initially, but then interrupted with dependent clauses until we come to the main clause at this sentence's conclusion, using the literary form *ella* (she) as the subject: *ella mi toglie e rende*.

*E **lei**, quando pur scalda, giova e offende*
el cor mio stanco, e fra dolci martiri
l'alma, qual uom che or ami et or s'adiri,
*in un momento **ella mi toglie e rende**.*

And **she**, when she also burns, uses and riles
my tired heart and, with sweet martyrdoms,
my soul, that man she would now love and bind,
in a moment, **she takes and rips me apart**.

It is with this type of holistic reading that we begin to develop a critical appreciation of Pico's poetic achievements, even though earlier critics have downplayed the quality of Pico's poetry.

CRITICAL JUDGEMENTS OF PICO'S SONNETS

In 1894, Father Felice Ceretti quotes the earliest biography of Pico, that by his nephew Giovanni Francesco II, Pico della Mirandola, in developing his critical appraisal of Pico's sonnets:

> With an elegiac song, with the sound of his own words, he had played with his loves, whom he had given over to the fires, which were written in five books, for the sake of religion; He played many of the same rhythms to the Hittites, which for the same reason consumed a match of fire.[38]

Ceretti continues on labeling the sonnets as *scarsissimi*, which might mean *very few*, but as we proceed here, we see the sense is either *the poorest* or *the leanest*, attributing the form and content of Pico poetry to the fact that "the poems of Petrarch in that day were in the mouths of everyone taken by love."[39]

Ceretti concludes in referring to great Italian writers:

> … such genuises, disdaining to write in their mother tongue, preferred that of Lazio – that the poetry and prose written in the vernacular pleased only simple people, with the Quattrocento a century of lethargy for Italian literature.[40]

With Ceretti we have a priest who over four-and-a-half centuries later still tows the party line and won't accept *il volgare*. Written 1894, such a narrow, parochial and erroneous judgment flies in the face of historical reality. As Francesco De Sanctis clarifies in his essential *Storia della Letterature Italiana* from a generation earlier in 1870:

> That same energy that threw the European Crusades in Palestine, and later pushed them towards India and to find America, now pushed the Italians to exhume the civil world that had been under Barbarian ashes. That language was their own – that knowledge was their own knowledge.[41]

De Sanctis describes the literary aspect of this new culture as "obvious." And, we have to say that the Quattrocento vernacular poets and writers of note, both male and female, are such as Leon Battista Alberti, Giovanni Cavalcanti,

Lorenzo de' Medici, Angelo Poliziano, Luigi Pulci, Matteo Boiardo, Lucrezia Tornabuoni, Antonia Pulci, along with the nascent scientific prose *Notebooks* of Leonardo.

If Ceretti diminishes Pico's poems, a century later Giorgio Dilemmi characterizes them as "questions, hypotheses, warnings, exorations, meditations and judgments." He goes on to say that Pico does not seem interested "in the really amorous sections, those of a sighing heart, which nurture the better part of lyrics, in a special way after Petrarch." Since Pico was a philosopher, Dilemmi contends he was drawn to "reason and assessment, and not to feeling and hearing." Dilemmi concludes that because of these things, "it is impossible to remove the sensation of a composite and unresolved attempt."[42]

Moreover, Dilemmi points out close similarities between lines in Pico and in Petrarch. Yet, the process of Pico creating an individual sonnet would belie the premise that he is deliberately mimicking specific lines in Petrarch. First, the process of creation within a given rhyme scheme would require more spontaneity than a mere *cut & paste* approach would allow. Second, although Pico admired Petrarch, as we discussed above, Pico did see his limitations as a poet "who has something to entice in the first instance, but does not satisfy further…" Indeed, we might confirm Petrarch does seem to slowly move "in the void his luminous wings in vain."

Third, the universal feeling of love, with all of its varieties of emotion and its relatively standardized metaphors, would make such similarities between lines of Pico and Petrarch more coincidental than direct referrals. Pico and Lorenzo de' Medici saw Petrarch as an earlier monumental poet, but not as an absolute, since they lived at a time where the relatively recent past was being eclipsed with new creative genius, of which they were a part.

Armando Torno judges simply that "the reader of the *Sonnets* will not discover Pico is a great poet, but will find in them a cultured man who loved poetry."[43] A swing and a miss! This judgment is absolute and reductionist, missing the intrinsic value an attentive and senstive reading can find in Pico's sonnets.

And, value there is.

Pico, young, bold and brilliant, was an original thinker, scholar, theologian and poet. He examined and rejected the deep context of the status quo. He crafted adaptable original poetic expressions that bear his own unique stamp, where the form embodies the content. His style was his own and might have evolved further had he lived longer. He *might have* expanded his sonnet sequence and even stepped into something other than what his first attempt led him to.

READING PICO'S SONNETS

In Sonnet 7, Pico uses a straightforward narrative in *loose sentences* where we see both the power and destruction that his haughty but inviting Lady holds over him, with him losing part of his reason. It is a description embodied through a picture of his crying eyes, as red as painted ivory, filled with tears that crescendo from a brook to a river, and then a lake.

> *Un sguardo altero e vergognoso e vago,*
> *un minio che uno avorio bianco pinge,*
> *gli ochi mei stanchi a lacrimar suspinge*
> *mutandoli in un rivo, un fiume, un lago.*

> A glance haughty and shameful and enticing,
> a red minium that paints white ivory,
> my tired eyes pushed to tears
> changing into a brook, a river, a lake.

In the next quatrain, while his eyes gaze upon his lady, he loses himself, pushed outside himself by her eyes and that arrow, both controlled by *Amor*:

> *E mentre lor contemplan l'altrui imago,*
> *perdo la propria, e for di me mi spinge*
> *el vigor di quei lumi ch'Amor tinge*
> *e 'l stral contra cui mai valse erba né mago.*

> And while they contemplate the other's image,
> I lose my own, and I am pushed outside myself
> by the power of those lights that Love controls
> and the arrow against which works neither potion nor magic.

While outside himself—indeed, not used here, but the very definition of *ecstasy*, with *ex* as *out of*, coupled with *stasis* as *standing*, as *standing outside oneself*— he cannot remember the reason for all this, his persona defeated by blind and passionate desire to the point that he loses feeling.

> *Così mentre si scorda la ragione*

*di sé, vincta dal cieco et amoroso
desio, qual uom rimango che non sente ...*

So while I forget the reason
of all this, defeated by blind and passionate
desire, I remain that man who does not feel ...

And, for certain, while Pico's heart suffers, it almost enjoys being trapped.

*e ben che 'l cor per ciò provi un noioso
stato, ben se ne dol, ma non se 'n pente,
quasi che goda de la sua pregione.*

and well that the heart for which it proves a difficult
state, suffers well from it, but not in shame,
for it almost enjoys its prison.

This struggle continues, with Pico losing all rationality in *Sonnet 17*, then regaining it, only to lose it again in *Sonnet 18*.

In the first six line of *Sonnet 17*, Pico asks his soul what it thinks. He then implores his reason to wake his spirit for his will is exhausted. Although his health is in good stead, reason's defense may not be ready. He continues by asking reason to enlighten the heart, which, by the way, is the seat of emotions, and his sense, whose ability it muzzles. Pico then intensifies this struggle over his self-control through the metaphor of a flimsy boat that races through a black storm.

*Che fai, alma? che pensi? Ragion, desta
lo spirto, ché la voglia è già trascorsa
là dove ogni salute nostra è in forsa,
se la diffesa tua non sarà presta;*

*aluma el core; el penser vago aresta;
Cosí fa' el senso, che punto lo smorsa.
O scogli, o mar falace, ove era corsa
la debil barca mia in sí atra tempesta!*

What are you doing, soul? What do you think? Reason, wake

the spirit, because the will is already spent
while all our health is in force,
if your defense is not ready;

enlighten the heart, stop the rambling thoughts;
the same to my sense, whose point you muzzle.
O rocks, false sea, where races
my weak boat in such a black storm!

In the first terzina, we see that Pico has regained self-control, his reason assured, with his inner eye aware of the potential dangers, with every wrong desire now gone. His mind, ready and strong, re-awakened to the good.

Da ora inanci fia piú l'ochio interno
acorto; ogni desir men bono è spento;
la mente accesa al ben, presta e gagliarda.

From now forward the inner eye will be
aware; every bad desire dead;
the mind awakened to the good—ready and strong.

In the final terzina, Pico tells God, not Apollo, not *Amor*, that he repents, telling him that in matters of love, people are weak from the first moment.

E se puncto te offesi, o Patre eterno,
perdoname, sí come io me ne pento:
sai che da' primi assalti om mal si guarda.

And if this point offends you, o eternal Father,
pardon me, even as I repent:
you know that from the first assault, a man looks sick.

In the very next poem, *Sonnet 18*, Pico uses a run-on sentence in the first quatrain to indicate that, once again, reason and his self-control are gone, that he has lost it, another torch inflames his heart, a new fire, begun by an old thought of love, destroys him *a dramma a dramma*. It is a testament to his poetic ability that he seemlessly blends the metaphors of the torch and fire into his own self-description.

Lasso, che un'altra face el cor m'enfiamma,
che gli ardenti desiri ivi rinova
e l'antiquo pensier, nel qual si cova
el foco che me struge a dramma a dramma.

Miserable me, for another torch inflames my heart,
that there renews burning desires
and the old thought, which nurtures
the fire that destroys me little by little.

In the next quatrain, Pico reflects back on his innocent youth with his mother, his soul a long way away from the current pain in his heart. He then implores his Lord, who tests him, but understands *Amor* and his fire.

Felici anni nei quai chiamava mamma:
longi dal mal in cor l'alma si trova!
Pietà di me, Signor, tu che per prova
intendi qual è Amor, qual la sua fiamma!

Happy years as a child calling my mom;
the soul long from pain in my heart!
Have mercy on me, Lord, you who to test
understands what is Love, what is his fire!

In the concluding terzinas, Pico asks his Lord if he should speak to his Lady while he sees Pico empty of heart, freedom and peace. It would please his Lord that Pico has faith and is no longer arrogant. In these six lines, the metaphors of *Amor*'s destruction become a reality that Pico struggles against.

E se talor con la mia donna parli,
per cui tuo fido amico andar si vede
privo del cor, de libertà e di pace,
piaciati noto apertamente farli
qual son gli affanni mei, qual è la fede,
quanto una mente altera a Dio dispiace.

And if sometimes you speak with my lady,

for which you see your faithful friend go
empty of heart, of freedom and of peace,
may it please you to know
what are my own troubles, what is faith,
how much a haughty mind displeases God.

Following the theme of Pico losing his reason, in Sonnet 41 he looks back upon his transformation from love. In the first quatrain, he describes how an *alta e suave* plague changed him, how *Amor* turned the key of his heart and then gave it to his Lady, his enemy.

> *Io me sento da quel che era en pria*
> *mutato da una piaga alta e suave,*
> *e vidi Amor del cor tôrme le chiave*
> *e porle in man a la nemica mia.*

> I feel changed from what I was before
> by a noble and courtly plague,
> for I saw Love turn the key of my heart
> and put it in the hand of my enemy.

In the second quatrain, Pico saw his lofty and pure Lady accept the key, after which she bound him in a way that was both fun and painful. Then, Jealousy guided him through the most depraved streets. Here, we see metaphor blend with Pico's experiences so that they are inseparable.

> *E lei vid'io acceptarle altera e pia*
> *e d'una servitú legera e grave*
> *legarme, e da man manca in vie piú prave*
> *guidarme occultamente Gelosia.*

> And I saw her accept it, lofty and pure,
> and bind me with a light and serious
> servitude—and Jealousy mystically guided me by
> the hand through the most depraved streets.

In the first terzina, Pico saw Reason leave and then new desires, thoughts and wants taking him over. It is fascinating to see how direct these lines become for the reader through Pico's personification of reason and his new emotions.

Vidi andarne in exilio la Ragione,
e desiderii informi e voglie nove
rate a venir ad alogiar con meco.

I saw Reason go into exile,
and new desires, thoughts and wants
suddenly come to live in me.

In this powerful concluding terzina, Pico blends the metaphors of prison, the departed personification of his soul and himself as a blind man as the ultimate fate of those who deal with love.

E vidi da l'antica sua pregione
l'alma partir per abitare altrove,
e vidi inanti a lei per guida un cieco.

And I saw from her ancient prison
my soul leave to live elsewhere,
and I saw before her as my guide a blind man.

I hope that readers find their own richness in Pico's verse, as I.

A NOTE ON THE TRANSLATIONS

Many people seem to read poetry in a desultory manner, often in *reader-response* mode as a very intimate and almost meditative process, as an active embrace of something *other*, one that is far removed from the fast-paced rush of everyday life in our demanding industrial and technological world.

These are readers who are not seeking any sense of authorial intention or historical context, but simply, in one way or another, pleasure, provocation, escape, enlightenment, confirmation or simply joy with words. No matter what, if any, all or none of these, this introduction and the notes are intended to help readers begin to understand Pico's forty-five sonnet sequence. My intent here is that these poems can be read, understood and enjoyed as if each sonnet were an occasional poem to stand by itself with readers jumping about them as they come to know the poems. Or, one can read them as part of a linear process with a focus on the entire sequence from start to finish.

My reading of the sonnets places the *io*, the first person subject *and author* of the poems, not as some ahistorical abstraction, but fully as Giovanni Pico della Mirandola himself. Given the then historical tradition of writing sonnet sequences as begun by Francesco Petrarca with his *Rerum vulgarium fragmenta*, which was certainly nudged along by the *Stilnovisti* and Dante with his own lyric poems and the *Vita nuova*, the case can be made, as Dilemmi has done, that Pico's sonnets are emulations of that tradition. However, I have taken a different path in the way that I read these poems for—because of the intensity and immediacy of the feelings, plus the emotions and personal reactions to what Aristotle would call *reversals*—there is interpretive evidence here to consider the *io* as Pico himself and these poems as *originals*.

My first goal is to provide as direct as possible meaning of the Italian into English with Pico's poetically archaic and colloquial language.[44] In order to decipher meaning, most readers will have to go back and forth between the original Italian, the translations, the notes and back again. As such, in the main, these notes are not progressive. There is some repetition so that readers can feel confident in stepping into the sequence wherever they want. For instance, Pico often uses *el* instead of *il*—easy enough to remember—but I point this out whenever he uses *el* to make the personal reading process more user friendly. Above all, the idea, then, is not a quick fix with these notes, but process of engagement with the original text.

My next goal was to provide some commentary on some of my translations themselves. As Benedetto Croce explains, the problem with translation is *faithful ugliness and deceitful beauty*.[45] Often literal translations can make for ugly reading in the translated language, while beautiful poetic renderings often bear no resemblance to the original. I hope to fall on the plus side.

My final goal was to avoid any definitive conclusions in the commentary, such as, "Pico is really discussing *x, y and z* here," because such a statement causes students to read the poems looking for those things while ignoring the totality of the poetic experience. This latter point is especially true in today's *cut & paste* student culture where reading, analysis and synthesis into a conclusive experience is supplanted by the quick Google search of dubious sources resulting in *non sequitur* responses by students. And now we have *AI* able to write papers, with students not thinking at all.

With this in mind: *festina lente*.

Bibliography

Alighieri, Dante. *The New Life of Dante Alighieri*, trans. by Charles Eliot Norton. New York: Houghton Mifflin, 1896.
Argan, Giulio Carlo. *Storia dell'arte italiana*, vols. 2 & 3. Firenze: Sansoni, 1981.
Bertolini, Lucia. *De vera amicitia. I testi del primo certame coronario*. Modena: Pannini, 1993.
Burke, Peter. *The Italian Renaissance: Culture and Society in Italy*, 3rd ed. Princeton: Princeton University Press 2014.
Busi, Giolio and Raphael Ebgi. *Giovanni Pico della Mirandola Mito, Magia, Qabbalah*. Torino: Einaudi, 2014.
Celenza, Christopher S. *The Intellectual World of the Italian Renaissance*. New York: Cambridge University Press, 2018.
Ceretti, Father Felice. *Sonetti Inediti del Conte Giovanni Pico della Mirandola Messi in Luce*. Mirandola: 1894; reprinted by Nabu Press, 2013.
Cirigliano, Marc A. *Melancolia Poetica: A Dual Language Anthology of Italian Poetry 1160-1560*. Leicester, UK: Troubador Publishing Ltd., 2007.
Cole, Alison. *Italian Renaissance Courts: Art, Pleasure and Power*. London: Laurence King Publishing, 2016.
Commissione municipale di storia patria e di arti belle. *Memorie storiche della città e dell'antico ducato della Mirandola*. Mirandola: Gaetano Cagarelli, 1876. Internet Archive. Accessed June 3, 2023, https://archive.org/details/memoriestoriche01itagoog/page/n237/mode/2up?q=Arezzo.
Copenhaver, Brian P. *Magic and the Dignity of Man: Pico della Mirandola and His Oration in Modern Memory*. Cambridge, MA: Belknap Press of Harvard University Press, 2019.
_____. "Giovanni Pico della Mirandola," *Stanford Encyclopedia of Philosophy*. Accessed July 16, 2023, https://plato.stanford.edu/entries/pico-della-mirandola/.
Croce, Benedetto. *Aesthetic as Science of Expression and General Linguistic*, trans. Douglas Ainslie. New York: Noonday Press, 1922.

D'Ancona, Alessandro and Orazio Bacci. *Manuale della Letterature Italiana*, v. 2. Firenze: G. Barbèra, 1929.
De Mauro, Tullio. *Grande dizionario italiano dell'uso*. Torino, UTET, 1999.
de' Medici, Lorenzo. *Canzoniere*, ed. by Paolo Orvieto. Milano: Mondadori, 1984.
de' Medici, Lorenzo. "Comento del magnifico Lorenzo de' Medici sopra alcuni de' suoi sonetti," *Opere*, v. 2, ed. by Attilio Simion. Bari: Laterza, 1914. Accessed Nov. 11, 2022. BEIC, https://it.m.wikisource.org/wiki/Opere_(Lorenzo_de%27_Medici)/II._Comento_del_magnifico_Lorenzo_de%27_Medici_sopra_alcuni_de%27_suoi_sonetti.
Derrida, Jacques. *Of Grammatology*, trans. by Gayatri Chakravorty Spivak. Baltimore: John Hopkins University Press, 1976.
De Sanctis, Francesco. *Storia della Letteratura Italiana*, v 1. Milano: Rizzoli, 1983.
D'Ovidio, Francesco. *Versificazione italiana e arte poetica medioevale*. Milano: Hoepli, 1910.
Edgren, Hjalmar, assisted by Giuseppe Bico and John Lawrence Gerig. *An Italian and English Dictionary, With Pronunciation and Brief Etymologies*. New York: Henry Holt and Company, 1904.
Gallelo, Gianni, *et al.* "Poisoning histories in the Italian renaissance: The case of Pico Della Mirandola and Angelo Poliziano," *National Library of Medicine*, May 2018. Accessed Feb. 3, 2023, https://pubmed.ncbi.nlm.nih.gov/29609050/.
Di Girolamo, Costanzo. *Manualetto di metrica italiana*. Rome: Carocci, 2021.
Farmer, S.A. *Syncretism in the West: Pico's 900 Theses (1486)*. Tempe, AZ: Medieval and Renaissance Texts and Studies, 1998.
Hunt, Dr. John M. "The status of the artist in renaissance Italy," in *Smarthistory*, May 14, 2023, https://smarthistory.org/the-status-of-the-artist-in-renaissance-italy/.
La fuga d'amore di Pico della Mirandola. Abumnews.net, January 2015. Accessed Feb. 2, 2023, https://www.albumnews.net/2015/01/la-fuga-damore-di-pico-della-mirandola/.
Musa, Mark. *Petrarch Canzoniere*. Bloomington: Indiana University Press, 1999. Kindle.
Petrarch, Francesco. "On the Nature of Poetry to his Brother Gherardo," *Familiar Letters*, from James Harvey Robinson, ed. and trans. *Petrarch: The First Modern Scholar and Man of Letters*. New York: G.P. Putnam, 1898. In the *Hanover Historical Texts Project*. Retrived Nov. 2, 2022, https://history.hanover.edu/texts/petrarch/pet13.html.
Petrocchi, Policarpo. *Novo Dizionario Scolastico della Lingua Italiana dell'uso e fuori d'uso*. Milano: Trèves, 1899. *Internet Archive*, https://archive.org/details/novodizionarios00petrgoog/mode/2up.
_____. *Novo dizionario universale della lingua italiana*. Milano: Trèves, 1887. *Internet Archive*, https://archive.org/details/novodizionarioun01petruoft.
Pico della Mirandola, Giovanni. *Lettere*, ed. by Francesco Borghesi. Firenze: Olschki, 2018.
_____. *Sonetti*, ed. by Giorgio Dilemmi. Torino: Einaudi, 1994.
Pico Della Mirandola, Giovanni (nephew). *The Life of Pico della Mirandola*. trans. by Thomas More, ed. by J. M. Rigg. London: David Nutt, 1890, 37. Published by the

Ex-classics Project, 2011. Accessed May 28, 2023, https://www.exclassics.com/Pico/pico.pdf.

_____. *The Life of Pico della Mirandola*, ed. and trans. by Brian P. Copenhaver, with Michael J. B. Allen. Cambridge: Harvard University Press, 2022.

Pomilio, Mario. *Petrarca e l'idea di poesia: Una monografia inedita*, ed. by Cecilia Gibellini. Roma: Studium, 2016. Kindle.

Powell, J. G. F. "10. Hyperbaton and register in Cicero," *Colloquial and Literary Latin*, ed. by Eleanor Dickey and Anna Chahoud. Published online by Cambridge University Press: 04 April 2011. Accessed April 15, 2023, https://www.cambridge.org/core/books/abs/colloquial-and-literary-latin/hyperbaton-and-register-in-cicero/7BDC02B6FE229CB5735D76279B54494D.

Procacci, Ugo. "L'uso dei documenti negli studi di storia dell'arte e le vicende politiche ed economiche in Firenze durante il primo Quattrocento nel loro rapporto con gli artisti," *Donatello e il suo tempo, Atti Dell'VIII Convegno Internazionale di Studi sul Rinascimento*. Firenza-Padova: Istituto nazionale di studi sul rinascimento, 1966, 11-40.

Rowland, Ingrid D. *From Heaven to Arcadia: The Sacred and the Profane in the Renaissance*. New York: NYREV, 2005.

Steiner, George. *Real Presences*. Chicago: University of Chicago Press, 1989.

Torno, Armando. "Viaggio all ricerca di Pico," in *Giovanni Pico della Mirandola, I Sonetti*, ed. by Gabriella Sica. Milano : La vita felice, 1996.

Walter, Ingeborg. *Lorenzo Magnifico e il suo tempo*, trans. Roberto Zapperi. Roma: Donzelli, 2005.

Sonnets

1
Dagli occhi de Madonna el solfo prende
Amore, et ha per mantici i desiri
vani: el cor soffia un vento de sospiri,
che in me, che stopia sum, la fiamma incende.

E lei, quando pur scalda, giova e offende
el cor mio stanco, e fra dolci martiri
l'alma, qual uom che or ami et or s'adiri,
in un momento ella mi toglie e rende.

Cosí di lode e di lamenti io strido,
e nel mar navigando senza remo
longe da lito, a salvo porto arrivo.

Cosí ridendo io piango e in pianto rido,
temendo io spero e nel sperar piú temo,
moro vivendo e poi morendo io vivo.

1
From the eyes of my lady, love takes
coals and pumps my empty desires through his
bellows: the heart blows a wind of desires
that in me—who am mere stuble—ignites the flame.

And she, when she also burns, uses and riles
my tired heart and, with sweet martyrdoms,
my soul, that man she would now love and bind,
in a moment, she takes and rips me apart.

So, of praise and lamentation I scream,
and in the sea sailing without oars,
long from shore, I arrive at a safe port.

So, laughing I cry and in tears I laugh,
fearing I hope and in hope I am more afraid,
I die living and then dying, I live.

2
De doe trece racolte in crespi nodi
Amor fe' el laccio che me avolse al collo,
e poi lo strinse, sí che nulla pòllo
soglier, se Morte non sia che lo snodi.

Dal lume de quegli ochi, che in tal modi
gitta talor, che invidia move Apollo,
reacesse il pecto dentro, e sí avampollo,
che sol di suspirar par che lui godi.

Gli acti suavi, inizio del mio male,
ché i marmi fan di cera l'arte maghe,
furon quel cun qual me involò a me stesso.

Le belle acorte parolette vaghe
nel cor se l'anidaro, che poi spesso
per volar d'indi indarno spiega l'ale.

2
With two tresses gathered in frizzy tangles,
love made a snare that he wrapped around my neck
and then tightened, so that nothing can
loosen it, if Death were not there to untie it.

From the light of those eyes, that sometimes cast
in such ways, so to move Apollo to envy,
reigniting inside the breast and burning it,
so that he seems only to enjoy yearning.

The charming actions—the beginning of my illness,
because the sorceresses' art makes the marble into wax—
were those that wrapped me into myself.

The beautiful, clever, enticing little words,
if they nested in the heart, often then explain,
in order—in vain—to fly from there, the wings.

3
Amor, che gli ochi mei facti han dui fiumi,
a nova piaga piú non resta loco,
e sí distructo m'ha l'antico fuoco,
ch'altra fiamma non ha che piú consumi.

El dir, che per cangiar e' fier costumi
d'altrui s'affaticò già tanto, è roco;
el viso in contemplar colei è fioco,
ch'abaglia noi, benché p'ogni altro alumi.

E pur m'aventa una nova ferita
Amore, e un'altra face che piú m'arda;
né l'empietà d'altrui a dir mi move,

né men belleza vòl ch'ancor io guarda.
Cosí par che riposso el cor non trove,
s'Amor, Madonna, o Morte non me aita.

3
Love, who made my eyes two rivers,
no longer remains here by the new wound,
and the ancient fire has so destroyed me
that another flame hasn't but to consume me more.

Speech, in order to change those fierce habits
of others, already exhausted itself so that it is hoarse;
sight, in contemplating her becomes weak,
which dazzles us, although, more than any other, illuminates.

And, as well, Love hurls a new wound at me
and another makes me burn more;
neither does the irreverence of what others say move me,

nor does beauty want me less to still look.
So it seems my heart finds no rest
if Love, My Lady or Death don't help me.

4
Dapoi che doi begli ochi, che mi fanno
cantar del mio Signor sí novamente,
avamparo la mia gelata mente,
si volge in lieta sorte il secondo anno.

Felice giorno, che a sí dolce affanno
fu bel principio, onde nel cor si sente
una fiamma girar sí dolcemente,
che men beati son che in celo istanno!

L'ombra, le piume e la pigricia e l'ocio
m'avean conducto dove la piú parte
è di color di cui non si fa stima,

ma Amor mi scorsi a piú degno negocio.
E se dolce ad alcun par la mia lima,
Madonna è quella, e non l'ingegno o l'arte.

4
Since those two eyes, that make me
sing of my Lord anew,
ignited my frozen mind,
my happy fate begins its second year.

Happy day at such a beautiful beginning
with such breathlessness, whence I felt a flame turn
so sweetly in the heart—
less blessed are those in heaven!

The shadow, feathers, laziness and my eyes
had led me where the greater part
are those we do not value,

but Love gave me a better deal.
And if my verse seemed so sweet to some,
Caused by My Lady—and neither genius nor art.

5

Amor, focoso giacio e fredda face;
Amor, mal dilectoso e dolce affanno;
Amor, pena suave et util danno;
Amor, eterna guerra senza pace.

Amor, tetro timor, speme fallace;
Amor, bugïa, fraude, sdegno e inganno;
Amor, false promesse, che l'uom fanno
gioir del mal come d'un ben verace.

Amore, amaro felle, amaro asenzio;
Amor, vane speranze e van desiri;
Amor, roco parlar, longo silenzio.

Amor, faville, lacrime e sospiri;
Amor, segnor crudel piú che Mezenzio,
che gode sempre de gli altrui martiri.

5

Love, fiery ice and cold torch;
Love, most loving illness and sweet breathlessness;
Love, sweet pain and helpful wound;
Love, eternal war without peace.

Love, dark anxiety, false hope;
Love, lie, fraud, disdain and deceit;
Love, false promises, that make man
Enjoy suffering as if it's a true good.

Love, bitter bile, bitter absinthe;
Love, empty hopes and empty desires;
Love, rough speech, long silence.

Love, fantasy, tears and laments;
Love, a master crueler than Mezenzio
who always enjoys the suffering of others.

6
Quando del sol la corruscante lampa
risplende, e quando a noi la nocte viene;
quando di neve son le spiage piene,
quando Zefir di fior le pinge e stampa,

quel mio nimico da cui uom mai non scampa,
per farme viver sempre in doglia e in pene,
cun lumi, laci, stral, fiamme e catene
mi piglia, punge, lega, abaglia, avampa.

E se talor di quei pensier io m'armo,
che sí forte mi fan, ch'io giurerei
d'esser piú forte che mai petra o marmo,

súbito poi, né come dir saprei,
ardo qual cera e me stesso disarmo,
in soccorso d'Amore e danni mei.

6
When the shining lamp shines
from the sun and the night comes to us:
when the shores are full of snow,
when Zephyr paints and gives form to them with flowers,

he my enemy from whom man never escapes,
in order to make me live in pain and punishment,
with lights, snares, arrows, flames and chains
he takes me, stings me, binds me, blinds me, inflames me.

And if sometimes I arm myself with these thoughts
that make me so strong that I would judge myself
being ever stronger than stone or marble,

soon, then, as I would not know how to say,
I melt that wax and disarm myself,
in the care of Love and my injuries.

7

Un sguardo altero e vergognoso e vago,
un minio che uno avorio bianco pinge,
gli ochi mei stanchi a lacrimar suspinge
mutandoli in un rivo, un fiume, un lago.

E mentre lor contemplan l'altrui imago,
perdo la propria, e for di me mi spinge
el vigor di quei lumi ch'Amor tinge
e 'l stral contra cui mai valse erba né mago.

Cosí mentre si scorda la ragione
di sé, vincta dal cieco et amoroso
desio, qual uom rimango che non sente;

e ben che 'l cor per ciò provi un noioso
stato, ben se ne dol, ma non se 'n pente,
quasi che goda de la sua pregione.

7

A glance haughty and shameful and enticing,
a red minium that paints white ivory,
my tired eyes pushed to tears
changing into a brook, a river, a lake.

And while they contemplate the other's image,
I lose my own, and I am pushed outside myself
by the power of those lights that Love controls
and the arrow against which works neither potion nor magic.

So while I forget the reason
of all this, defeated by blind and passionate
desire, I remain that man who does not feel;

and well that the heart for which it proves a difficult
state, suffers well from it, but not in shame,
for it almost enjoys its prison.

8
Dapoi che me convien in altra parte
volger i passi e pur lassar colei
che a pianger ne commove a invidia i dei,
che 'l nostro cor divise in mille parte,

l'alma nostra non già da qui si parte,
anzi rimane in compagnia di lei
ch'odí piatosamente i sospir mei,
e sol di noi se 'n va la piú vil parte.

Ferma speranza, immaculata fede,
memoria d'una mente altera e pia,
un amoroso desio, un giacio, un fuoco,

un vago lume, ove d'Amor se vede
la forza, un dolor longo, un breve gioco
sempre saran cun me, Donna, fra via.

8
Since I must turn my steps
elsewhere and leave she who
moved the gods to jealous tears,
so that our heart broke into a thousand pieces,

our soul doesn't leave here
but remains in the company of she
who mercifully hates my cries
and only our most vile part goes away.

Still hope, immaculate faith,
memory of an ethereal and pure mind,
an amorous desire, an ice, a fire,

an engaging light where one sees Love's
power, a long suffering, a brief game
are always with me, Lady, on my journey.

9

Io preso sono come un pesce in rete,
come ucello che ai rami l'ale invesca,
e son posto in pregion né vedo und'esca,
né men son pur mie voglie ardite e lete.

E sí com'io bevesse al fondo Lete,
di me mi scordo e par che non m'incresca
l'infelice mio stato, anzi s'infresca
ognor dal vagagiar la ingorda sete.

Dolci sospiri e dolce ogni tormento,
dolce le doglie son, dolci gli affanni,
dolce el pianto, el languir, dolce el lamento:

tanto può Amor cum soi fallaci inganni!
Tal, mal mio grado, al nostro mal consento,
e lui ringrazio ancor poi de mei danni.

9

I am taken like a fish in a net,
like a bird with wings entangled in branches,
then I'm put in prison where I can neither see nor escape,
nor less are my burning and happy desires.

And even if I were to drink from Lethe's spring,
I would have no memory and that would seem not to increase
my unhappiness, but would always refresh
my great thirst for the chase.

Sweet sighs and sweet each torment,
sweet are the wounds, sweet the breathlessness,
sweet the tear, the suffering, sweet the lament:

Love can so deceive with his lies!
Such, my ill state, I agree to our illness
and I thank him again for my wounds.

10
Amor m'ha posto como al giogo el bue,
como al sol brina, e son qual uom ch'è privo
di sentimento, e s'el sia morto o vivo
de iudicar ne sta spesso intra due.

Tanto può in me con le bellezze sue
quel bel viso legiadro, altero e divo,
de cui piangendo in tante carte io scrivo,
adombrandone el stile or una or due.

Ma tu, fiero Fanciul, perché disciolta
lassi andar lei e ognor piú stretto leghi
el cor, che fu legato un'altra volta?

Perché non li comandi, o non la preghi
che, mentre l'alma è nel corpo sepolta,
premio alla nostra servitú non neghi?

10
Love has placed me like the ox to the yoke,
as the frost to the sun and I am a man devoid
of feeling and, if one might judge, either
dead or alive, often between the two.

So much inside me with her beauties
that beautiful face, graceful, ethereal and divine,
of which I write crying on so many pages,
my stylus darkening them, now one, then two.

But you, fiery Youth, why do you let
her go free and every moment more tightly bind
my heart that was yet bound another time?

Why don't you command her or beseech her
for that—while my soul is buried in the body—
reward for our servitude you don't deny?

11
Ch'io languisca tuttora amando quella
di cui la viva imagine, ch'io scolpo
ne la mia mente afflicta, und'io mi spolpo,
fa che 'l spirto dei membri mei si svella,

no 'l Cel, non la Fortuna o la mia stella,
non quel da cui discese el mortal colpo
qua giú nel cor, non la mia donna incolpo,
ma solo el Mastro che la fe' sí bella.

Quivi el vigor, quivi la sua potenzia,
quivi mostrò sue forze manifeste,
quivi l'arte, l'industria, la prudenzia;

quivi mostrò come un spirto celeste
coprir se può, per sua onnipotenzia,
sotto mortal, caduca e fragil veste.

11
That I suffer still loving one whose
vivid image—that I sculpt
in my afflicted mind where I flay myself—
makes the spirit of my body awaken,

neither Heaven, nor Fortune nor my star,
not that from which lowers the mortal blow
here down into my heart, not my innocent lady,
but only the Master who made her so beautiful.

Here his vigor, here his power,
here he showed his manifest strengths,
here art, industry, prudence;

here he showed how a celestial spirit
is able to cover, through its omnipotence,
a fleeting and fragile garment with mortality.

12
Ochi, fate el terreno umido e mole
dove il polve segnò collei col passo,
ch'or fa vostro vigor, fugendo, casso,
che in quel che non è lei oprar non volle.

Piangete, rivi, piangete, ombroso colle;
pianga ogni sterpo, ogni virgulto e sasso,
in compagnia del cor languido e lasso,
che Madonna nel suo partir ne tolle.

Piangete, Ninfe e voi che nel paese,
Driade, sete; e tu, arïa, piagne
per la partita del tuo chiaro sole.

Pecto, suspira; e tu, mia lingua, lagne;
orechie, non odete piú parole:
da ogn'altra voce voi serete offese.

12
Eyes, make the earth moist and soft
where the dust marks her step,
that now makes your vigor, fleeting, empty,
not want to do anything that is not her.

Weep, rivers, weep, shady hill;
Cry, every tree stump, every twig and rock,
in the company of the suffering and tired heart,
that My Lady in her leaving removed.

Cry, nymphs and you in the country,
Dryads, thirst; and you, air, weep
on the parting of your clear sun.

Breast, sigh; and you, my tongue, whine;
ears, do no longer hear words:
from every other voice you will be offended.

13
Or su, ponette mo ne la Fortuna
vostre speranze, o miseri mortali,
che a l'uom, quanto piú vola, tarpa l'ali,
facta di bianca in un momento bruna!

Cosa ferma non è sotto la luna!
E poi che fra sí pochi beni e frali
cagion è un viver longo a tanti mali,
felice è chi de vita è spento in cuna.

O almanco, mentre el celo è amico a noi,
compire alora la giornata nostra
è meglio che aspetare in sin a sera.

O quanto è amaro a l'uom a dir – Io foi! –
E certo apertamente ne 'l dimostra
quanto sia cieco chi nel mondo spera.

13
Come on, put your hopes
in Fortune now, oh—miserable mortals—
for to a man, the more he flies, his wings are clipped—
a bright fact in a dark moment!

Nothing certain under the moon!
And so among so few riches and fragile
changes is a long life with many sorrows,
happy is one with a life spent in the cradle.

Oh, at least, while the heavens are our friends,
then our day is done,
which is better than waiting into the night.

Oh, bitter it is for man to say—I was!—
And certainly openly demonstrates
how blind is he who hopes in this world.

14
S'io vi guardo, Madonna, el vigor che esce
de quei lumi leggiadri mi fa un sasso;
se gli ochi altrove io volgo o a terra abasso,
manco qual tracto fuor de l'unda pesce.

Cosí ogni nostro operar a mal riesce,
e son già del passar sí vinto e lasso,
che sol de non aver al primo passo
compíto el mio camino el me rincresce.

Io ne adimando a Amor spesso consiglio,
che, mal per me, fui süo, se l'antica
sua medicina al cor infermo offende;

et ei par che a l'orechia, al cor mi dica:
– Gemina el sguardo, e non sera' im periglio:
fura nel primo, e nel secondo rende. –

14
If I look at you, My Lady, the power that comes from
those graceful eyes make me a stone;
if I turn those eyes elsewhere or lower them to the ground,
I lack strength just like a fish out of water.

So every action of ours brings pain
and I'm already past such defeat and exhaustion
that I only regret not taking the first step
of my journey.

I often ask Love for advice,
which, bad for me, I was his, thus his
ancient medicine upsets the sick heart;

then he appeared at my ear and said to my heart:
"Double your gaze and you won't be in danger:
steal with the first, and in the second, give back."

15
Poi che l'alma mia luce al ciel è gita,
ove ogni altra parer fa vile e obscura,
misero me infelice, che piú dura
esser cosa a me può che stare in vita?

Perché seco là su non è salita
che in amarla qui pose ogni sua cura?
Aspra Morte, che sempre el meglior fura
su la piú verde etate e piú fiorita!

Gli occhi leggiadri e quel bel viso adorno,
le man di fresca rosa e bianca neve
or polve sun, che nulla cura o sente.

Cosí tutti alla terra fan ritorno:
però chi spera in cosa cosí breve
sempre, ma tardo spesso, se ne pente.

15
As the light of my soul went to heaven,
so every other thing seems vile and dark,
miserable me unhappy—so what harder
thing might there be than continuing to live?

Why hasn't my soul ascended up there with her
as it took every care in loving her here?
Harsh Death who always steals away the best
to up there, the greenest and most flowered summer!

The graceful eyes and that lovely face,
hands of fresh rose and white snow
are now dust, that cares for or feels nothing.

So all make the return to earth,
yet he who always waits for something
so brief, often later, regrets it.

16
Ecco doppo la nebia el cel sereno
che invita li uccelletti andare a schera;
ecco la luce che resplende ove era
di caligine opaca dianci pieno.

Afligice mo, Invidia, aspro veneno
a cui t'alberga! abassa la tua altera
testa, ché chiunque alfine in Dio non spera,
presto ne veni ogni sua forza al meno!

Carità cun Iustizia e intera Fede,
che sempre furno a me fide compagne,
secur mi fan de chi fra via m'assale;

e mentre el cor, ch'è in me, da lor se vede
acompagnato andar, poco gli cale
di che altrui rida, o di che alcun si lagne.

16
Here after the fog is the clear sky
that bids the little birds to fly in formation;
here the light shines where it was
full of dense haze before.

Now afflicting, Envy, bitter venom
lives in you! Lower your raised
head, for whoever in the end doesn't believe in God,
quickly every power of yours comes to nothing!

Charity with justice and complete Faith,
who were always my faithful companions,
keep me safe from whoever assaults me on the road;

and while my heart, that is in me, sees me
accompanied by them, heats up little
when others might mock or some might whine.

17
Che fai, alma? che pensi? Ragion, desta
lo spirto, ché la voglia è già trascorsa
là dove ogni salute nostra è in forsa,
se la diffesa tua non sarà presta;

aluma el core; el penser vago aresta;
Cosí fa' el senso, che punto lo smorsa.
O scogli, o mar falace, ove era corsa
la debil barca mia in sí atra tempesta!

Da ora inanci fia piú l'ochio interno
acorto; ogni desir men bono è spento;
la mente accesa al ben, presta e gagliarda.

E se puncto te offesi, o Patre eterno,
perdoname, sí come io me ne pento:
sai che da' primi assalti om mal si guarda.

17
What are you doing, soul? What do you think? Reason, wake
the spirit, because the will is already spent
while all our health is in force,
if your defense is not ready;

enlighten the heart, stop the rambling thought;
so do the sense, whose point you muzzle.
O rocks, false sea, where races
my weak boat in such a black storm!

From now forward the inner eye will be
aware; every bad desire dead;
the mind awakened to the good—ready and strong.

And if this point offends you, o eternal Father,
pardon me, even as I repent:
you know that from the first assault, a man looks sick.

18
Lasso, che un'altra face el cor m'enfiamma,
che gli ardenti desiri ivi rinova
e l'antiquo pensier, nel qual si cova
el foco che me struge a dramma a dramma.

Felici anni nei quai chiamava mamma:
longi dal mal in cor l'alma si trova!
Pietà di me, Signor, tu che per prova
intendi qual è Amor, qual la sua fiamma!

E se talor con la mia donna parli,
per cui tuo fido amico andar si vede
privo del cor, de libertà e di pace,

piaciati noto apertamente farli
qual son gli affanni mei, qual è la fede,
quanto una mente altera a Dio dispiace.

18
Miserable me, for another torch inflames my heart,
that there renews burning desires
and the old thought, which nurtures
the fire that destroys me little by little.

Happy years as a child calling my mom;
the soul long from pain in my heart!
Have mercy on me, Lord, you who to test
understand what is Love, what is his fire!

And if sometimes you speak with my lady,
for which your faithful friend sees you go
empty of heart, of freedom and of peace,

may it please you to know
what are my own troubles, what is faith,
how much a haughty mind displeases God.

19
Che bisogna che piú nel mar si raspe,
fra tante frode e fra sí falsi inganni?
Parca, depone el fin a tanti affanni,
qual si sia quella che 'l mio fato inaspe!

Da l'erculëo freto al fiume Idaspe
si sa como abia perso i mei verdi anni
in adorar colei, che nei mei danni
si gloria, a mie pregher' sorda qual aspe.

Sino gli ucelli, i fiummi, i monti e campi
san como suspirando si distempre
il pecto stanco e como il cor avampi;

san como Amor e in che diverse tempre
senza pietà me incenda con doi lampi:
donque meglio è morir che languir sempre.

19
What good is more flailing at sea
among so many frauds and such false deceptions?
Death, lays the end with so many pains
that must be my unexpected fate!

From the Herculean sea to the Hydaspes River
everyone knows how I lost my youth
in adoring her, she who revels in my
wounds, that viper deaf to my pleas.

Since the birds, the rivers, the mountains and fields
know how my tired, suffering breast
dissolves and how my heart enflames;

they know how Amor, in many different moods,
mercilessly burns me with two flames:
therefore, better to die than languish forever.

20
Se non spenge el mio fuoco el fiume eterno
ch'Amor versa da gli ochi, e il piancto molto
se 'l desir cresce, e lo sperar m'è tolto,
e tuttavia m'afflige el caldo interno;

se 'l Cel, se la Fortuna, se l'Averno
me son rebelli, e se nel cor mio stolto
ognor vomi del furor cieco e sciolto
qual giglio o rosa in prato al tempo verno;

se un sdegno altero, un'ira, un disprezare
altrui senza cagion è per mercede
del mio servire, el lamentar non vale.

Se non s'apreza una sincera fede,
Anima, dimmi, che debiam noi fare?
– Temer di pegio, et or languir nel male. –

20
If the eternal river does not quench my fire
that Love pours from the eyes and if my desire
grows my tears a lot and hope is taken from me,
and still my hot insides plague me,

if Heaven, if Fortune, if Hell
are rebels to me, and if, in my foolish heart,
I were to vomit every hour from the blind and unleashed fury
that lily or rose in the meadow at wintertime,

if a haughty disdain, an anger, a scorn
from others without cause is the reward
for my service, complaining is not worth it.

If sincere faith is not valued,
Soul, tell me, what should we do?
"Fear the worst and now languish in suffering."

21

Io temo che a lingua non consenta
el cor, che forse piú ca neve agiaccia;
io temo non intrar in cotal traccia
che poi d'eservi entrato io me ne penta.

E se adesso ardi, da qui a puoco spenta
fia forse la tua fiamma, e chi te alaccia
che sa che di te soglier non gli piaccia,
e Amor reponga el stral che or aventa.

Chi sa che l'oro in piombo non se muti,
ch'i gagliardi tuoi preghi fervidi, anzi
sera sian piú che pietra inerti e muti.

Però bisogna oprar miglior bilanzi,
ch'io so como ogni cosa se tramuti
e un fior disecca, che fiorí pur dianzi.

21

I fear that my heart does not agree with
my words, which perhaps freeze more than snow;
I fear not entering a path
that then entered I would regret.

And if now you burn, from this moment your flame
will be only be a little lessened, for who binds you
knows that freeing you does not please him—
and then Love aims the arrow that he now shoots.

Who knows if gold doesn't turn to lead—
because of your strong, fervent prayers, rather
they will be more inert and dumb than stone.

But we must reach the best balance—
I know how every thing transforms
and a flower dries up that bloomed just before.

22
Qual uomo a cui el papavero con l'oppio
furato ha i sensi, per lo freddo troppo
tal io rimasi a lo amoroso intoppo,
agiacciando nel fuoco ond'io ne scoppio.

E quando ch'io vi vedo el mal radoppio,
e se io tento fugirmi di galoppo,
manco nel primo passo qual bue zoppo,
e a forza e mei co' bei vostri ochi acoppio.

Quinci l'antica piaga se rinfresca,
ch'a noi advien che pur di novo incespi
là dove el sulevarmi piú m'incresca.

Cosí a lacio dei biondi capei crespi
legato Amor terrami in la sua tresca,
fin che vechieza el nostro volto increspi.

22
That man from whom the opium poppy
has stolen his senses, in the oh-so-cold
I was so stuck in the amorous trap,
freezing in fire where I was exploding.

Then when I see I the ancient sickness redouble
that if I try to gallop away,
I miss my first step like a lame ox
and forcibly couple your beautiful eyes with mine.

Hence, the old plague resumes
by coming to us as new trap
there where exciting me sparks me the more.

So, the curly blond tresses
tied by Love drag me into his plot,
until old age wrinkles our face.

23
Se Amor è alato come el è depincto,
perché in me fermo, lento, sede e giace?
Se gli è piciol fanciul, perché gli piace,
vincitor, stringer l'uom poi che l'ha vincto?

Se agli ochi porta un bianco velo avincto,
come sí certe manda le sue face,
per cui l'aflicto cor, che se disfece,
consumar vegio a morte e quasi extincto?

Se voler può, che fa del suo cavallo?
Se gli è signor, perché va scalzo e nudo?
Perché par dolce et è nel fin sí amaro?

Dimel, ti prego, o singular e raro
Francesco, onor de l'acidalio ludo
e primo e sol ne l'apollineo ballo.

23
If Love is winged like in the paintings,
why does he lie in me still, slow, set?
If he is a tiny child, why does he like—as
victor—to squeeze the man he has defeated?

If he wears a white blindfold over his eyes,
how does he send such well aimed torch-like glances
with which he strikes a heart that unravels
that I see consumed to death, almost wiped out?

If he can fly, why does he need a horse?
If he is a lord, why does he go barefoot and naked?
Why does he seem sweet, but, in the end, so bitter?

Tell me, please, o singular and rare
Francesco, pride of the Acidulous game of Venus,
and the one and only in the Apollonian dance.

24
Non sono in Aeti cervi o lepor tante,
né credo in Ibla ancor tant'ape siéno,
né tante erbe ebbe mai nel vago seno
Cerere, o fior sopra le chiome errante;

né tante selve son sul monte Atlante,
né mai de tante fronde arbor fu pieno,
di pesce el mar, di stel'el ciel sereno,
quante cure nel cor d'un cieco amante.

Quanti son li martiri, affanni e guai
che le misere piaghe versan sempre,
ben sa chi 'l prova et io no 'l dico invano.

Ma pur che Amor cun puoco dolce tempre
l'aspro venen, non se n'acorge om mai
fin che vechio non è col capo cano.

24
There are not so many deer or hare on Mount Athos,
nor do I believe on Mount Ibla still so many bees,
nor many herbs ever in the elusive heart of
Ceres, nor flowers above the wandering foliage;

nor are many forests on Mount Atlas,
nor trees full of ever so many fronds,
fish in the sea, stars in the calm sky,
as many cares in the heart of a blind lover.

So much are the pains, gasping and trouble
that the miserable plagues always pour forth,
he well knows who seeks it and I don't say in vain.

But as long as Love tempers with a little sweetness
the bitter venom, one never notices,
not even in old age, not even with a grizzled face.

25
Qual stral, qual rapto vento non precorre
el veloce girar del ciel, che sgombra
quanto qua giú el cel riscalda e adombra,
om, dimi, che qui vòi tua speme porre?

Non sai che non se può dal mondo tôrre
l'esser fallace, che i cor ciechi ingombra?
Non sai che passarem qual fumo et umbra?
ch'ogni cosa terrestre a morte corre?

Ma poi che per tal lege a lei per forza
andar conviente, come va ogni rio
al mare o come cosa grave al centro,

oprar tu dèi che sol di te la scorza
seco ne porti, ma quel che v'è dentro
ritorni ad abitar là dove uscío.

25
What arrow, what ravishing wind is not ahead
of the fast turning sky, that clears
as much down here as the sky heats and darkens,
man, tell me, that here you put your hope?

Do you not know that you cannot take from the world
the false being that clutters blind hearts?
Do you not know that we will pass that smoke and darkness?
That rushes every earthly thing to its death?

But then by such law you must
go to her, as each river goes
to the sea or as a serious thing to the core,

you must plan that she gets only your
mortal body, but that which is inside
returns to live there where it came from.

26
Se 'l basso dir di mei suspir in rima,
i quali Amor ne la età mia aprile,
per segregarme dal vulgo piú vile,
tra' da parte del cor secreta et ima;

e se la nostra inculta e roza lima,
se 'l mio cantar e 'l mio debile stile
può meritar, ben che inornato e umile,
nome fra quei di che fa el mondo stima,

non vo' mi guidi di Latona il fio
a' fonti aganippei, o di sua insegna
Callïopè m'adorni, Euterpe o Clio.

Ché nulla Musa e d'ogn'altra piú degna
in piú fresche aque e in piú onorato rio
mi bagna, e su nel ciel salir m'insegna.

26
If my lowly words of suffering in rhyme,
which Love would open in my life,
in order to separate me from the vulgar most vile,
to draw from the secret and deep part of my heart;

and if our uncultured and rough file,
if my weak song and style
may deserve, well that inornate and humble,
name among those who make world opinion,

I don't want you to guide me, son of Latona
to the spring of Aganippe or, to adorn me with their sign
Calliope, Euterpe or Clio.

Because no Muse nor any other worthy
bathes me in fresh waters and the most
honored river—and then teaches me to ascend up to heaven.

27

Se benigno pianeta ha in noi vigore,
io credo ben che tutto quel fu infuso
nel spirto che nel corpo tuo fu chiuso,
Madonna, in questo mondo inferïore;

e credo ancor che 'l nostro almo Factore
t'avria nel ciel tenuta per suo uso,
ma in terra ti mandò per far qua giuso
de sè fede, a me guerra, al mondo onore.

E credo ancora fermo, e ne son certo,
che 'l spirto non si doglia, anzi si gloria
dil tuo bel velo che lo tien coperto;

et io viva farò la lor memoria,
se 'l fonte dove aspiro mi fia aperto,
texendo del tuo nome eterna istoria.

27

If the benevolent planet has power in us,
I well believe that all that was infused
in your spirit as well as your body was closed,
My Lady, in this lower world;

and I believe still that our nurturing Creator
would have led you to heaven for his own use,
but on earth he sent you down here to do
his will: for me, war, for the world, honor.

And I still firmly believe, and I am sure of it,
that the spirit does not sorrow, but glories
in your beautiful veil that covers you;

and I will keep their memory alive,
if the source that I aspire to will be open,
weaving eternal history with your name.

28
Amor ben mille volte e cun mille arte,
come uom sagio che amico se dimostra,
temptato ha pormi ne la schera vostra,
che empieti de triunfi soi le carte;

ma la ragion di Lui m'era in disparte,
che la strata dil cel vera mi mostra:
Cosí l'uno pensier cun l'altro giostra
e 'l cor voria partir, né pur si parte.

Onde ancor né gioir nostra alma o trista
far può Fortuna, e furno in grande errore
gli ochi, se lo contrario a lor pareva.

Gelosia forse, che 'l nostro Signore
seguir suol sempre, offerse cotal vista
al cor, che di Madonna alor temeva.

28
Love, well a thousand times and with a thousand arts,
as a wise man and my friend demonstrated,
he has attempted to put me in your ranks,
which completed his triumphs predicted by the Tarot;

but his reason was keeping me apart,
so the layer of true heaven shows me:
thus one thought jousts with the other
and my heart wants to leave, but it does not.

Where again Fortune is able to make our soul
neither joyous nor sad and my eyes were
in great error, since the contrary appeared to them.

Jealousy perhaps, that usually follows
our Lord, offers such a view
to my heart that then feared my Lady.

29

Tolto me ho pur davanti agli ochi el velo
per cui bon tempo non mirai ben dritto
e mi celò le carte ove è descritto
per qual strata ir se può presto nel celo.

E vedo ben che può mia fede in zelo
presto mutar quel ch'era già prescritto,
né mai perdon disopra fu desditto
a l'uom, pur che nel mal non cangi pelo.

Et io ne son exempio al popul tutto,
che, cun lor caminando, in breve spazio
al commun precipizio era condutto.

Nel fin cridai, del vanegiar già sazio;
– Perdon, – e di tal voce nacque un frutto
che l'alma trasse dallo eterno strazio.

29

I also took the blindfold from my eyes
because for a good bit of time I didn't aim straight
and it hid the card where it tells
what level I can reach in heaven.

And I well see that my zealous belief in what
was already foretold can quickly change,
not ever to pardon above what was denied
to man, though in evil he never changes his ways.

And I am an example to the all the people,
who, walking with them on a short path
to city's precipice, was led.

In the end I cried out, already sated with raving,
"Pardon," and from such a voice a fruit was born
that the soul pulled from eternal torment.

30
Spirto, che reggi nel terrestre bosco
i nostri piè per questo cal selvagio,
guarda, quando serà fornito el viagio,
non dica el tuo Factor: – Non te conosco.

Io ti fei puro e bianco et or sei fosco
da caligine operto è 'l vivo ragio;
pascer ti volse non di querci o fagio
ma d'ambrosia, e da un angue hai tolto el tòsco.

Sordido sei e maculato e cieco,
e piú mi sdegno essendo tu nostra opra:
però parte nel ciel non avrai meco. –

Dunque mentre gli piace che ti copra
questo mio vel, deh fa che sempre seco
esser possàn nel regno là disopra.

30
Spirit, who in the terrestrial forest controls
our feet in this wild glade,
look—when the journey will be provided,
do not tell your Maker: "I do not know you.

I made you pure and white, and now you are cloudy
grey, labored is the living light;
I wanted you to graze not on oak or beech
but on ambrosia, and you have taken the poison from a serpent.

You're dirty and spotted and blind,
and I'm more sorry you're our creation:
however, you will not be with me in heaven."

Hence, while he likes to cover you
with my veil—alas—he does it so
we can always be with him in the kingdom up there.

31
Amore, a che bisogna piú ti sforzi
trarmi cun gli altri a l'amoroso gioco?
Del vanegiar non men sazio che fioco
già son, né temo a servirti mi sforzi.

So come presto un fiato solo amorzi
d'ogni nostra fortuna un lieto foco,
come un piacer terren può durar puoco,
come ogni uom morte di sua spoglia scorzi.

E voi, che Amor seguite, date un stroppio
a' lacci, alle catene, e l'amo e l'esca
rimanga senza preda exinanita.

E già di noi, che rimembrandol scoppio,
seria fata insanabil la ferita;
ma curata ho la piaga essendo fresca.

31
Love, to what need must you insist
on drawing me and others into this game of love?
By now neither am I less sated than weak from the raving,
nor do I fear serving you as I struggle.

I know how quickly a single breath dims
the happy fire of our fortune,
how a terrestrial pleasure can last only a little,
how every dead man is stripped of his shell.

And you—who follow Love, give a cripple
to the ropes, chains, and the hook and bait—
remain exhausted without prey.

And already remembering us and the explosion,
serious was the incurable wound;
but I have cured the plague becoming fresh.

32
Se ellecto m'hai nel cel per tuo consorte,
Segnor, fa' non mi tenga Amor piú a bada,
né per me indarno aperta sia la strada
del cel e de Pluton rotte le porte.

Sai come sopra noi regna la Morte,
come el dí sette volte el iusto cada,
come un piacer terreno ai sensi agrada,
come io son fral, come 'l nemico è forte.

Tu sai, Signor, che me su la tua stampa
formasti con mirabil magistero
e spirasti nel volto a me la vita;

donque d'amor, di fé el mio core avampa
e cercami, s'i' vo fuor del sentero,
come un pastor la peccora smarita.

32
If you have chosen me as your consort in heaven,
My Lord, neither hold me to Love's bidding,
nor in vain open the way for me
to heaven or break the doors to Pluto.

You know how Death reigns over us,
as justice falls seven times a day,
as an earthly pleasure delights the senses,
as I am as frail as the enemy is strong.

You know, Lord, that you formed me on your model
with admirable skill
and you breathed life into my face.

So, of love, my heart burns with faith
and look for me, if I go am beyond the path,
as a shepherd who has lost his sheep.

33
Poi che 'l gran Re dil celo alla sua stampa,
l'alma creò nudata d'ogni vizio,
a' nostri eterni danni un pors'inizio,
chi furar volse la febëa lampa.

Quinci Colei, da cui uom mai non scampa,
scese nel mondo e in alto precipizio
guida chi del gran primo benefizio
grata memoria non riscalda e avampa.

Costei miete ogni cosa, altro che 'l nome,
e 'l suo fatal, irreparabil colpo
deprecar non si può cun doni o censi.

Costei nel cor, ne gli ochi ora mi scolpo,
che apertamente mi dimostra come
obedir den, non commandar, i sensi.

33
From the moment the Great King at his press
created my soul stripped of every vice,
a fated beginning to our eternal damnation
to whoever wanted to steal the Phoeban lamp.

Hence, she—from whom man never escapes—
descended into the world and from a high precipice
guides who doesn't boil or burn from
the welcome memory of the first great gift.

This lady harvests everything, other than your name,
and you cannot ward off
her fatal, irreparable blow with gifts or incense.

This lady in my heart, in whose eyes I now try to exonerate myself,
who openly shows me how
I must obey, not command, my senses.

34
Quando io penso talora quel ch'era anzi
l'alma al Principio suo fosse conforme,
ch'io non pensava l'onesto, lo enorme
doverse misurar cun par bilanzi;

e che quando l'uom crede el gli avanzi,
spesso el sol cade, e lui el gran sonno dorme;
né che secarsi e diventar può informe
súbito un fior che verdegiava dianzi;

non me acorgeva, dico io, ahimè infelice,
esser qui in viaggio, esser qui posto in bando,
altrove esser la patria e la mia stanza.

E mentre e' mie' passati error pensando
men vo, fermo nel cor l'alte radice
de Carità, di Fede e di Speranza.

34
When I sometimes think of what it was before
my soul was conformed to its Essence,
I did not think the honest, the enormous
would have to be measured as a balanced pair;

and that when a man believes he is advancing,
often the sun sets and he sleeps deeply;
he becomes arid and does not know
suddenly a flower bloomed in front of him;

she did not notice me, say I, alas, unhappy,
here on a journey, placed here in exile,
somewhere else being my homeland and my home.

And while I must think less of my past
mistakes, I hold in my heart the lofty roots
of Charity, of Faith and of Hope.

35

Chi va del mondo lustrando ogni parte
dove si colca e dove el sol piú luce,
ritrovarà che a le terrestre luce
el ben col mal varia fortuna parte;

ma, lasso, che me offende in ogni parte,
né mai sopra di me vien chiara luce.
Verson lacrime sempre le mie luce,
e piú quando altri possa o 'l sol si parte;

né men quando al ritorno scuote l'umbra,
mentre el sudor distilla in qualche libro
del caldo a cui non trovo aure né umbra.

E quando ben mio stato penso e libro,
vorrei nel viaggio a Stigge esser in umbra,
essendo in fiamma uno exsicato libro.

35

Whoever goes in the world illuminating every part
where the sun sets and shines bright,
will find that with terrestrial light
the good with the bad changes with fortune;

but—oh my!—what offends me in every place,
never does a clear light shine above me,
my eyes always pour tears,
and more so when others go to bed and the sun departs;

nor less when it jolts the darkness with its return,
while dread condenses in some book
from a heat where I find neither auras nor darkness.

And when I well ponder my state and the book,
I would like my trip to the Styx to be in darkness,
being a dried book in flames.

36
Era la donna mia pensosa e mesta,
vòta di gioia, carca di dolore
e cun lei insieme ragionava Amore,
ch'a meza nocte a lacrimar me desta,

quando ignudo gli apparve senza vesta,
a guisa de un mesaggio, el nostro core
per farli scusa del commesso errore,
se 'l promesso errore ancor s'aresta.

Ella a pietà non ch'e perdon si volse,
ché per farla piú certa del suo stato
el cor scopersi: le sue fiame e i strale

ne l'umido suo grembo alor racolse,
e l'empio mio Segnor, che gli era a lato,
disse: – Volato è qui con le mie ale. –

36
My woman was pensive and sad,
empty of joy, loaded with sorrow
then Love was speaking with her,
at midnight crying awoke me,

when naked he appeared to her without clothes,
in the guise of a messenger, our heart
would excuse the committed error,
if the promised error would stop.

She asked for pity from who would not pardon,
because to make it certain she would
discover the state of his heart, its flames and arrows

drawn then into her moist womb,
and my cruel Lord, who was beside her,
said, "He has flown here with my wings."

37
Sí como del mondo umbra senza luce,
posta del mondo alle piú inferne parte,
Cosí riman tu, Italia: ecco si parte
el tuo vivo splendor ch'altrove or luce.

De' soi bei raggi aviva le tue luce
mentre che a' Galli e a noi suo lume parte,
che quando tutta vòlta in altre parte
serà, rimanga in te la impresa luce.

Alor me parerai como del cieco
regno di Dite stano i spirti bui,
ché si cognosce un ben quando è perduto.

E quando il danno tuo fie cognosciuto,
intenderai s'avia da pianger teco,
dicendo: – Io non son piú quella ch'i' fui. –

37
Thus, as darkness without light
goes to the most infernal parts of the world,
so you remain, Italy: here now departs
your lively splendor that elsewhere is now light.

Your eyes give life with his beautiful rays,
while for the Gauls and for us his light leaves,
so when everything will have turned toward other
places, may the intended light remain in you.

Then, you will appear to me as the dark spirits
belong to the blind realm of Dis,
because one knows something good when it is lost.

And when your damage will be known,
you will understand if I begin to cry with you,
saying, "I am no longer who I was."

38
Per quel velo che porti agli ochi avinto
e per colei che si creò ne l'acque,
pel bel paese ove la Ninfa nacque
per cui fusti da te legato e vinto;

per la faretra di cui vai accinto,
pel strale a cui el mio cor per segno piacque,
per la vendetta de cui mal non tacque
di te, ch'indi ne fui poi quasi extinto,

Amor, deh move il stral, che in ocio siede,
accuto piú che mai contro a costei
che 'l tuo bel nome e la mia vita adumbra:

tal che o per prova al nostro mal díe fede
o io no 'l senta; o al fin, se iusto sei,
o me soleva o l'uno e l'altro ingombra.

38
For that blindfold that you wear bound to the eyes
and for she who was created in the waters,
for the beautiful country where the Nymph was born,
for whom you were bound and defeated;

for the quiver for which you are prepared,
for the arrow for which my heart liked to be a target
for the vendetta for which evil did not keep silent
about you—from all that I was almost extinguished,

Love, alas, moves the arrow that rests in my eye,
more severe than ever against she
who darkens your beautiful name and my life:

therefore, either try to have faith in our illness
or I won't survive it—for, in the end, if you are right,
either I am used to it or both of us are finished.

39
Chiara alma, chiara luce, chiaro onore,
chiara virtú, chiari costumi alteri,
chiaro intellecto, chiari desideri,
chiara nova beltà, chiaro splendore,

chiaro albergo di senno e di valore,
chiari, canuti e leggiadri penseri,
chiaro spirito e chiari magisteri,
chiara rosa vermeglia, chiaro fiore,

chiara gemma piú assai che un chiaro sole
quando apre l'anno verde, e rivi, colli
orna de fresche e palide vïole:

questi doni fe' Giove, e a ti donolli
per monstrar che lui può quanto che vòle;
per farne fede poi qua giú mandolli.

39
Clear soul, clear light, clear honor,
clear virtue, clear lofty manners,
clear intellect, clear desires,
clear new beauty, clear splendor,

clear dwelling of wisdom and value,
clear, cultured and elegant thoughts,
clear spirit and clear mastery,
clear pink vermillion, clear flower,

clear gem much more than a clear sun
when it opens the green season, and rivers, hills,
adorned with fresh and delicate violets:

these gifts made by Jove, and given to you
to show that he can as much as he wanted—
to show faith, then, he sent them down here.

40
Segnor, pensava in rime racontarve
ove prima ligato fu el mio core,
ove el mio pianto comenciò e 'l dolore
e fece Amor di me quel che a lui parve,

quando Apollo, segnor nostro, m'apparve
e disse: – Or canta d'un chiaro splendore
ch'aluma l'universo, e lassa Amore
che l'uom sempre lusenga in false larve.

Io ben del suo bel nome cantarei,
ma se ne sdegna e, facto emulo a nui,
spesso ad altrui mi fa parer men chiaro. –

Cosí lui a me; et io risposi a lui:
– Volenteri, Signor, te ubedirei,
se donato m'avesti un stil piú raro. –

40
Lord, I thought to recount to you in rhyme
where my heart was first bound,
where my weeping and pain began,
where Love did to me what he wanted,

when Apollo, our Lord, appeared to me
and said, "Now sing of a clear splendor
that lights the universe, and leave Love
that we always flatter with false illusions.

I would sing well of her beautiful name,
but if she scorns this and, after, emulates us,
it really makes me often appear less clear to others."

So, he to me; and I replied to him:
"Gladly, Lord, I would obey you,
if you were to have given me a better song."

41

Io me sento da quel che era en pria
mutato da una piaga alta e suave,
e vidi Amor del cor tôrme le chiave
e porle in man a la nemica mia.

E lei vid'io acceptarle altera e pia
e d'una servitú legera e grave
legarme, e da man manca in vie piú prave
guidarme occultamente Gelosia.

Vidi andarne in exilio la Ragione,
e desiderii informi e voglie nove
rate a venir ad alogiar con meco.

E vidi da l'antica sua pregione
l'alma partir per abitare altrove,
e vidi inanti a lei per guida un cieco.

41

I feel changed from what I was before
by a noble and courtly plague,
for I saw Love turn the key of my heart
and put it in the hand of my enemy.

And I saw her accept it, lofty and pure,
and bind me with a light and serious
servitude—and Jealousy mystically guided me by
the hand through the most depraved streets.

I saw Reason go into exile,
and new desires, thoughts and wants
suddenly come to live in me.

And I saw from her ancient prison
my soul leave to live elsewhere,
and I saw before her as my guide a blind man.

42

Pleona: Tremando, ardendo, el cor preso si truova.
Poeta: Ov'è la neve, il laccio, il foco, il sole?
Pleona: I tuoi sguardi, i dolci acti e le parole.
Poeta: Vòi taccia, chiuda gli ochi e non mi mova?

Pleona: Questo el mio mal non spinge, anze 'l rinova.
Poeta: Perchè?
Pleona: Perchè indi nascon tre parole:
virtú, stil, legiadria, unde non dole
fuoco, giaccio, catena, anzi gli giova.

Quel che lo lega, par la lingua snodi,
quel che l'agiaccia, de virtú lo incende,
l'arde in legiadre et amorose tempre.

Poeta: Donque meglio me vedi, miri et odi?
Pleona: Ben sai che sí, però che non me offende
agiacciando, stringendo, ardendo sempre.

42

Pleona: Fearing, burning, one finds my heart taken.
Poet: Where is the snow, the snare, the fire and the sun?
Pleona: Your glances, sweet acts and words.
Poet: Will you be silent, close your eyes and not move from me?

Pleona: This does not cure my illness, but rather, renews it.
Poet: Why?
Pleona: Because, from thence hid three words:
virtue, style, grace, whence not paining
fire, ice, chains—but rather, pleasing them.

That which binds him appears to be a snare of words,
that which freezes him, from its power ignites,
burning in a graceful and amorous temper.

Poet: Then better to see, admire and hear me?
Pleona: You well know it is so—however, they do not offend me,
freezing, grasping, burning always.

43
Era ne la stagion quando el sol rende
a' dui figli di Leda il bel offizio,
quando ch'io gionsi a l'umbra d'un ospizio
ove natura süe forze extende.

Ivi fra pedaglion, travacche e tende
gionse da l'alto ciel per artifizio
una Ninfa inmortal di tanto auspizio,
che solo il contemplar la vista offende.

Quivi era Apollo, Giove e gli altri dei
per rapir quella tutti, ma Cupido
cun Febo la legò per triunfarne.

Iove adirato el car salí per farne
vendetta, ma l'acorto amico e fido
s'ascose in vista, e se 'n fugí cun lei.

43
It was in the season when the sun makes
a beautiful sacrament to the two children of Leda,
when I arrived in the shadow of a hostel
where nature extends her forces.

There among pavilion, canopy and tent,
arrived quickly from the sky
an immortal Nymph of such eminence
that only thinking of looking at her offends.

Here were Apollo, Jupiter and the other gods,
all to ravish her, but Cupid
with Phoebus moved her to defeat them.

Jove, angry, ascended in the chariot to make
a vendetta of it, but my shrewd and faithful friend
saw this and fled with her.

44
Già quel che l'or'distingue, i mesi e gli anni,
i soi corser ne l'onde refrescava,
quando m'apparve, e so ch'io non sognava,
una Cerva che avea d'argento i vanni.

Doi cacciator ch'avean squarzati i panni
seguivan quella, e l'un sí glie monstrava
el mele, e l'altro so che la chiamava
dicendo: – Guarda costui non t'inganni! –

L'animaletto fermo in sé racolto
dubio, incerto stava, e pur al mele
che piú la se acostasse a me alor parve.

Et io de ciò me ne affannava molto
che me acorgea del ricoperto fele,
e mentre me ne doglio ella disparve.

44
Already that which time decides, the months and the years,
his horses refresh themselves in the waves,
when appeared to me—and I knew I wasn't dreaming—
a Doe with silver wings.

Two hunters who had quartered some hides
followed her and one so teased her
with an apple and I heard the other call her
saying, "Be careful he doesn't trick you!"

The dear little animal, stopped as it gathered in herself
doubt, remaining uncertain the more she
approached the apple—so it seemed to me.

And from that I became so breathless
that I became aware of being covered with bitterness
yet while this pained me, she disappeared.

45
Misera Italia e tutta Europa intorno,
che 'l tuo gran padre Papa iace e vende,
Marzoco a palla gioca e l'onge stende,
la Bissa è pregna et ha sul capo un corno.

Ferrando inferra e vendica el gran scorno,
San Marco bada, pesca e puoco prende,
la vincta Bissa ora San Georgio offende,
la Lupa a scampo veglia nocte e giorno.

Sega la grassa stracia in Mal avezi
e la Pantiera circondata crida,
femine e puti tien Romagna in pezi.

Da Aquile e Griffi al ciel ne va le strida,
e 'l ciel non ode, e regna Mori egipzi,
Tarquin, Sardanapal, Crasso e Mida.

45
Wretched Italy, and all throughout Europe,
Because your great father Pope sells his bed, because
Marzocco plays at ball and extends his claws,
the Bissa is pregnant and has horns for a hat.

Ferrando enchains and avenges the great humiliation,
San Marco watches, fishes and takes little,
the victorious Bissa now offends San Georgio,
the evasive She-Wolf on guard night and day.

The fat saw rips through with the usual Evil
and the surrounded Panther shrieks,
Romagna cuts women and babies to pieces.

From Eagles and Griffins the shrieking runs through the skies,
but the heavens do not hear and so reign the Egyptian Moors,
Tarquin, Sardanapalus, Crassus and Midas.

Notes on Pico's Sonnets

SONNET 1

1-3: Love takes burning coals from his lady's eyes which ignite his yearnings. Petrarch begins *RVF* with *Amore*, Love, who is Cupid all grown up as a man, with his bow and arrows, while Pico gets down to personal heated passion immediately.

Dilemmi points out that Pico begins his sequence in his very first sonnet with this phrase in his first line:

> Dagli occhi de Madonna…
> (From the eyes of my lady…)

This is similar to Petrarch's sonnet 348, a sonnet near then of the 366 poem *RVF*:

> Da piú begli occhi e dal piú chiaro viso…
> (From the most beautiful eyes and most beautiful face…)

It is a standard trope in love poetry that attraction comes from the lady's eyes, so, no copying Petrarch here. Further, Pico refers to his lady's eyes burning him "as coals," while Petrarch is "naked and blind." There is a direct emotional intensity in the Pico sequence that begins in this very first poem which is so different from Petrarch's studious, nuanced and verbally polished expressions. Petrarch talks of love, Pico of passion, arousal. We can conclude, then, that Pico breaks from repeating or even emulating Petrarch in order to tell his own story. Similarities between lines of Pico and Petrarch, then, are a coincidental use of vocabulary and tropes in *love poetry*.

1-2: *Dagli occhi de Madonna el solfo prende / Amore* emulates Latin's periodic style, where a word's ending determines it meaning, as opposed to English's use of *loose sentences*, where word order determines a word's meaning. The literal meaning of the Italian here is "From the eyes of [my] Lady the coals takes Love…" By placing *Amore* at the end of the phrase, *Amore's* agency is emphasized. A better translation is "From the eyes of my lady,/love takes coals …"

1: *Madonna* = derived from *mia donna* = *my lady* or simply *donna*. In French, we have *madame* = *ma* + *dame*.
1: *el*, a poetic form of *il*, with *e* a softer sound than *i*.
4: *sum* is Latin for *sono*. Pico uses Latin as expressions that are natural to him, that, as he moves on with his exploration of the sonnet, becomes a part of his poetic *koine*.

4-8: This quatrain is one Latinesque period, where the subject, *lei* does not meet its verb and direct object, until the second half of the fourth line, *mi toglie e rende*. One might consider this a stretch of the sense of the entire quatrain, but such composition makes the action here more descriptively complete and dramatically effective, with the action revealed at the end. It is analogous to Aristotle's statement in the *Poetics: 26*, where he presents one view whereby tragedy is considered more direct and simple for an uneducated audience, while epic poetry, requiring a long and certainly multiple sessions to complete, requires a more educated audience that understands the story's background and some of its nuances. (Aristotle then presents a counter argument in which he argues tragedy is superior.)

4-8: She takes, binds and pleases his heart and soul, which she then rips apart.
6: *el cor* instead of *il cuore*.
8: *ella mi toglie e rende*, a visceral and graphic conclusion of the first two stanzas.

9-11: Pico screams praise for his lady and laments his suffering, as a boat on the water without oars, a boat that finally reaches safety.

12-14: Love is a state of overwhelming emotional confusion embodied in oxymorons: laughing/crying; tears/laughing; fear/hope; in hope/more afraid; dying/living and finally, living. Here in the last *terzina*, Pico expresses the gamut of emotion from elation to despair, concluding with the stoic realization that as he writes *io vivo*, he must confront these conflicts in life. Thus, wounded, he carries on.

SONNET 2

1-4: While in emotional confusion in Sonnet 1, here Love entraps Pico tightly in a snare made of her hair, with only death unable to untie it. Death as liberator appears in 3:14, ... *Morte non me aita*, with *aita* as a poetical form of *aiuta*; while we read Death as ruler in 32:5, *Sai come sopra noi regna la Morte*.
1: *De doe trece = di due trecce*, with *de* meaning either *from* or, in a better sense here, *with*.
3-4: *pòllo / soglier = può soglierlo*.

5-8: The light from her eyes also makes Apollo enjoy desiring her.
6: *che invidia move Apollo* is a Latinate construction for *che muove Apollo ad invidia*, in order to fit the rhyme scheme and to place emphasis that even Apollo is moved by her.
7: *il pecto = il petto*.

9-11: A terzina with a Latinate paranthetical interruptor where the sense is *Gli acti suavi furon quei*.

12-14: Pico invokes his poetry in line 12 as the beautiful, clever, enticing little words.
12: *Vago* is difficult to translate because it means very different things: 1) vague, rambling, undefined. 2) eager or greedy. 3) attractive, graceful, lovely. 4) fond lover, admirer. Often, because the lover is lost, the translation could go any which way.
13-14: Another Latinate construction with a sense *[parolette] che poi spesso spiegano le ale*.
In English, the subject, verb and direct object read: *The beautiful, clever, enticing little words ... often then explain ... the wings*.

SONNET 3

1-4: Love makes him cry and opens new wounds.
Facti = fatti; dui = due; nova = nuova; loco = luogo; distructo = distrutto

5-8: Pico's speech and sighs become weak.
7: *el viso = il viso*.

9-11: New wounds hurt.
11: *move = muove*.

12-14: Love wants him to seek more. His heart can only find peace with the help of Love, his lady or Death.
11-12: *né ... né*, an enjambment meaning *neither ... nor*.
13: *el cor = il cuore*.

SONNET 4

1-4: Beginning its second year, his lady's eyes make him sing of love.
1: *doi* ochi= *due occhi*
1: *Dapoi che doi begli ochi* refers back to the first line of Sonnet 1: *Dagli occhi de Madonna ...*, so Pico develops the power of his lady's eye into a conceit, an idea that extends beyond a single poem.

5-8: He is happy, breathless, with a sweet flame in his heart—more blessed than heaven.

9-11: *The shadow*, away from the light of his lady, where *his poetry* is *lazy* or inadequate—things we should not value.
9: *le piume*, literally, *the feathers*, but here a reference to *the quill*, a writing instrument—hence, his poetry. *L'ocio = l'occhio*.
10: *conducto = condutto*.

12-14: Love helped him. His poetry was sweet to some, but not because of his ability, but rather, through his subject matter, his lady.
12: *negocio = negozio*.
13: *lima*, literally, a file, but here it means *poetry*. Dante begins a meme of referring to the writing of verse with the verb *limare*, to file or polish, which means both to *form* or *shape* poetry, but also that the substance of the poem is concrete, tangible; i.e., *significant*.

SONNET 5

The effects of love laid bare in this beautifully drawn poem, lyrical, yet pessimistic.

Amore (Love), in this poem as *anaphora*, the repetition of a word at the beginning of each phrase, or here, each line. In this case, *Amore* serves to introduce many of the oxymoronic guises of love, such as fiery ice, helpful wound, false promises, with each example of love as bringer of disappointment, as destroyer of happiness.

1-4: Love's effect on the senses.
1: *focoso giacio e fredda face* = ecstasy overwhelming the senses so that the fire of passion feels like ice and the hot torch of love feels cold. Note, *giacio* = *ghiaccio*.
2: *mal dilectoso e dolce affanno* = delicious evil and breathless after ecstasy.
3: *pena suave* = sweet pain, with ecstasy resembling pain.
4: *eterna guerra senza pace* = eternal war without peace anticipates the negative side of love; e.g., strife with one's lover, ruining peace of mind, the loss of reason, which we see in the next stanza and subsequent sonnets.

5-8: *Amore's* effect on the mind and social relationships.

9-11: *Amore's* conclusions, ending in bitterness, rough speech and long silence.

12: The two possibilities of *Amore* containing both positive and negative with the initial fantasy that ends in tears, that also encapsulates the various oxymorons such as a *helpful wound*,

13-14: *Amor* is crueler than Menzentius, an impious king of the Etruscans known for his extreme cruelty on the battlefield, eventually killed by Aeneas.

SONNET 6

1-4: In this context, day, night, winter and summer mean always or forever, poetically said with beautiful visual imagery.
2: *la nocte* = *la notte*.

5-8: People never escape the torments of *Amore*, who punishes in many ways, expressed here with two ancient aesthetic norms: *variety* and *copia*.

9-11: Pico attempts to reinforce himself against the negative effects of Love.

12-14: …but, that pretense, *qual cera* (that wax; i.e., that mask), he burns it away (*ardo*), coming from inside himself, an inevitability of Love's true power over his own will.
14: *in soccorso d'Amore e danni mei*, with *soccorso* as care in the sincere sense, but with the double edge sword of Love as pleasure and pain (*danni mei* = *danni miei*).

SONNET 7

1-4: Pico's lady asserts her power over him, beginning with a "haughty and shameful and inviting" glance.
2: *Minio* = a red paint used on then contemporary manuscripts and also as an underpainting for gold leaf in both fresco and panel painting. Here, painting white ivory with red pigment denotes ruining purity with passion, a remorse expressed in Pico's ever-growing tears from his bloodshot eyes.

5-8: While his eyes look at his lady, Pico stands outside himself, loses himself, his rationality, from her eyes, her beauty and also by Love's arrow.
6: *for di me* = *fuori di me stesso* = outside myself.

9-11: A key moment in the narrative of the sonnet sequence: Pico forgets his own reason through blind desire, then does not feel.

12-14: His heart suffers, but not in shame, almost enjoying the experience.

SONNET 8

Although Pico leaves his lady, his soul remains. Even though he still has *un amoroso desio*, with intense passion denoted by *un giacio, un fuoco*, he still suffers long, while the pleasures of love are *un breve gioco* = *un breve giuoco*, a brief game.

1-4: Pico must leave his lady, whose beauty moved the heavens to jealous tears.

5-8: His soul remains with his lady, as she mercifully hates his cries.

8: *dal vagagiar* = *dal vagghegiare* = to ogle or woo, with the sense here as part of an ongoing process; i.e., a pursuit or chase.

9-11: Hope, faith, memories of her loftiness—along with passion and desire, with fire and ice meaning intense physical passion—are with him...

12-14: ... as are *un vago lume*, a dim (or undefined) light of Love's power and along with it, suffering.
13: *breve gioco* = the brief pleasure of passion.
14: *cun me* = *con me*.

SONNET 9

With suffering as *un pesce in rete*, an entangled bird and Pico in prison, this poem is a series of metaphors or reality, for as Proverbs, 23:7 says, "For as he thinks in his heart, so is he."

1-4: Taken like a fish in a net or a bird entangled in branches, Pico is placed in prison with his burning desires.
4: *lete – liete.*

5-8: Even if he could forget by drinking from Lethe's waters, one of the five rivers of Hades, the one that causes the loss of all memory, he would still have an insatiable thirst through wandering.

9-11: Lots of sweet suffering.
10: *son = sono.*

12-14: Love deceives Pico through his lies, but he thanks him *"per mei danni."*
12: Interesting insertion of the Latin *cum* instead of *con.*

SONNET 10

1-4: *Amor* has put Pico like the ox to the yoke, devoid of feeling, and, so out of sorts, either dead or alive, or between the two.
1-2: Lovely metaphors here on struggle, the ox and yoke or the frost and sun.

5-8: Pico is so filled with her beauty, he cannot but write one page of verse after the other.
5: *Tanto può in me*, an elliptical phrase for *Tanto può* **essere** or **stare** *in me.*
8: Engaging turn of phrase, *adombrandone el stile or una or due*, literally, *darkening them the stylus, one then two.*

9-11: Pico wonders why love let his lady roam freely while he binds his heart that is already bound to her.
9: *fiero Fanciul = Amor =* fiery youth.

12-14: Pico, whose soul is buried in his body, wonders why *Amor* does not remind their lady to reward them for their servitude.

SONNET 11

1-4: Loving her who awakens his spirit, Pico suffers, flaying himself in his own mind.
3: *ne la mia* = *nella mia*.
4: *svella* = *sveglia*.

5-8: Love is behind it all.
5: *no 'l Cel* = *non il Cielo*.
8: *la fe' sí bella* = *la fece sí bella*.

9-11: *Amor* has vigor, power, strength, etc.
9: *potenzia* = *potenza*.
13: *onnipotenzia* = *onnipotenza*.

12-14: Love is celestial, incorporeal, but able to control the tangible, mortal world. Nifty for him.

14: A hyperbaton: *sotto mortal, caduca e fragil veste*, should read *caduca e fragil veste sotto mortal*.

SONNET 12

Pico entreats himself to feel his emotions.

1-4: Pico asks his eyes to cry to make the earth soft for *her* steps.
1: Ochi = occhi; *mole* = *molle*.
3: *ch'or* = *che ora*.
4: *lei oprar non volle* = *lei operare non vuole*.

5-8: He implores all of nature to weep because his lady took his suffering heart.
5: *colle* is a masculine noun *collo* meaning mountaintop, but made feminine to match the rhyme scheme.
8: *tolle* = *toglie*.

9-11: He tells the nymphs and dryads to cry for the parting of the sun, the bright sun, *chiaro sole*, a metaphor for his lady.

12-14: He asks his breast to sigh, his tongue to whine and his ears to be deaf to

words—they are offended from outside voices; i.e., all that matters is her, nothing else.
12: *Pecto* = *petto*.

SONNET 13

This poem is *memento mori*, a reminder of one's mortality.

1-4: Pico reminds that Fortune rules human destiny: *che a l'uom, quanto più vola, tarpa l'ali*= to a man, the more he flies, his wings are clipped.
1: *mo* = *mò*, now.
2: *l'uom* = *l'uomo*.
4: *facta* = *fatta*.

5-8: Nothing is certain but sorrow.

9-11: As long as the heavens smile upon us, we can rest safely over night.
9: *almanco* = *at least*.

12-14: Bitter experiences, unfulfilled dreams, make reflecting on one's life difficult.
12: A conundrum in understanding, for Dilemmi (p. 28) transcribes *io foi* as *io fui*, the literary form of "I was." The sense here could mean simply that he is narrating something in the past. Or, perhaps more distinctly, he is making a statement about his existence, as if to defiantly say, "I am," in the face of opposition, but here, in the past as "I was."

SONNET 14

1-4: Pico's lady's eyes weaken him.
1: *el vigor* = *il vigore*.
3: *abasso* = *abbasso*.
4: *tracto* = *tratto*.
4: *manco quel tracto fuor de l'unda pesce* is a hyperbaton, a not normal word order, and also an ellipsis. Literally, *I lack that trait outside of the wave fish*. The sense is: *manco quel tracto [come un] pesce fuori dell'unda* = I lack strength just like a fish out of the wave (or water).

5-8: Every action we take brings pain, but Pico regrets not starting his journey.
6: *son* = *sono*.

7: *sol = solo*.
7-8: *el me rincresce* = I regret it.

9-11: *Amor's* advice is bad for Pico.
9: *adimando = io addomando = io domando*.
10: *süo = suo*, with a dieresis over the *u* to denote that the dipthong *süo* counts as two syllables, not the usual dipthong counting as one.

12: *ei = egli*.

12-14: *Amor's* advice is to take from his lady and then give back to her.
13: *im = in*.
14: *fura = furare* = to rob or steal.

SONNET 15

1-4: Pico's love went to heaven, so all seems dark.

5-8: Pico laments that death has not taken him up to the *etate piú fiorita*.
5: *seco = con se*.
8: *etate = estate*.

9-11: Pico's lady is gone, all is dust.
11: *or polve sun = ora sono polvere*.

12-14: Everyone returns to earth, but waiting for brief pleasure is regretful.
12: *fan ritorno = fanno ritorno*.

SONNET 16

1-4: After fog clears, little birds fly and clear light shines where haze before.
1: *la nebia = la nebbia*; *el cel = il cielo*.
2: *a schera = a schiera* = in formation or in a group.
4: *dianci = dinanzi*.

5-8: The bitter venom of envy lives in you. If you do not believe in God, your power comes to nothing.
5: *afligice mo = affligge ora*.

6: *abassa* = *abbassa*.

9-11: Charity, justice and faith always accompanied Pico.
9: *cun* = *con*.
11: *secur* = *sicuro*.

12-14: In him, his heart sees his companions, but it heats up when others mock or whine about him.
12: *el cor* = *il core*.
12-13: *el cor ... da lor se vede/acompagnato andar* = my heart, that is in me, sees I must be accompanied by them.

SONNET 17

In the first two stanzas, Pio asks Reason to wake the spirit and enlighten the heart. In the first terzina, lines 9-12, Pico gathers inner strength with his mind awakened to the good, with bad desires now dead. In the last terzina, Pico asks *Amor* for forgiveness for going contrary to his plan.

1-2: Pico entreats *Ragion*[e] (Reason) in this poem, *Ragion, desta lo spirito*, to wake the spirit, asleep from (10) *ogni desir men bono*, every less good desire.

Earlier in the sequence, in Sonnet 7:9-11, Pico writes, *Cosí mentre si scorda la ragione/di sé, vincta dal cieco et amoroso/desio*, where he forgets his reason because of blind and passionate desire. Later, in Sonnet 41: Pico writes of reason going into exile while new desires, thoughts and wants come to live in him, *Vidi andarne in exilio la Ragione,/e desiderii informi e voglie nove/rate a venir ad alogiar con meco*.
3: *forsa* = *forza*.

5: *aluma el core* = *illumina il core* = enlighten the heart, something Pico entreats reason to do.
5: *el penser vago* = *il pensiero vago*, with *vago* here denoting vague, rambling or undefined. Although one of its other alternative meanings relating to *attraction* or *graceful* might be a stretch.
5-6: *el* = *il*.
7-8: Pico summarizes what he has been through to this point, with his self metaphor as *la debil barca*, a weak boat, in *mar falace*, false seas with a black storm, where the adjective *atra* able to mean either *black* or *horrible*.

9-12: A turning point for Pico, where his *occhio interno* becomes aware of what has so far transpired.
9: *inanci* = *innanzi*.
10: *acorto* = *accorto*.

12-14: Pico asks *Amor* for foregiveness.
12: *puncto* = *punto*; *Patre* = *Padre*.
14: *om* = *uomo*; *mal* = *male*.

SONNET 18

In Sonnet 17, Pico seems to have resolved the problems love posed for him, but he is again taken as *another torch inflames* [his] *heart ... renews burning desires*, with *the old thought*, with *the fire that destroys me little by little*.

1: *lasso* = tired, weary, unhappy, yet, the sense in this quatrain, a complete sentence, the sense is stronger—hence, a more intense translation as *miserable*.
1: *el cor m'enfiamma* = *infiamma il mio cuore*.
3: *l'antiquo pensier* = *l'antico pensiero*.
4: *el foco* = *il fuoco*.

5-6: Pico remembers the carefree innocence of his earliest years, *felici anni*, with his mother.
7-8: *tu che per prova/intendi qual è Amor* = *tu, che mi prova, intendi qual è Amor*.
8: *qual la sua fiamma* = ellipitcal for *qual è la sua fiamma*.

9-14: Line 9, *E se talor con la mia donna parli* is the dependent clause, while line 12, the first line of the final terzina, is the main clause, *piaciati noto apertamente farli*, which is a deferential elliptical phrase to *Amor*, [I hope that] *it may it please you to know*.
13: *mei* = *miei*.

SONNET 19

Pico expresses the futility of his suffering with love, with death at the end. Everyone knows he lost his youth through her, that all nature knows he is tired, how *Amor* burns him so that it is better to die.

1: *Che bisogna* = literally, *what need*, but with the emotional intensity and in the

colloquial tone of Pico, the sense is *what good*; *si raspe* = colloquial for *si raspa* (*raspare*) = *to rasp, scrape, scratch, paw*, but here, as a metaphor for Pico in the middle of the water, a better sense is *to flail*.
3: *Parca* = one of the three *Parcae* from Ancient Roman religion. Here, Dilemmi clarifies, as *death*. *El fin* = *il fine*.
4: *inaspe* = an adjective derived from the verb *innaspare* = *to hesitate, get confused* or *be puzzled*. Hence, another possible translation might be *puzzling* instead of *unexpected*.
6: *como* = *come*; *abia* = *abbia*; *mei* = *miei*.

9: *sino* = until.
10: *san* = *sanno*; *distempre* = colloquial for *distempra* because of the rhyme scheme.
11: *pecto* = *petto*; *como* = *come*; *avampi* = *avvampi*.

12: *tempre* = *tempera*.
13: *doi* = *due*.
14: *donque* = *dunque*.

SONNET 20

The variety and *copia* of Pico's suffering in the first 11 lines. The final terzina explains that sincerity will not save him.

1-11: An example of *anaphora*, with each phrase introduced by *se*, creating a long compound dependent clause that begins with the first line, *Se non spenge el mio fuoco eterno* and concludes with the main clause in line 11 with *el lamentar non vale*.
1: *el* = *il*.
2: *da gli ochi* = *dagli occhi*; *piancto* = *pianto*.

5: *Cel* = *Cielo*.
5: *Averno* = the pagan word for underworld, the Christian one is Hell.
7: *ognor* = *ognora*.
8: *verno* = *inverno*.
10: *cagion* = *cagione*.

12: *s'apreza* = *s'apprezza*.
13: *debiam* = *dobbiamo*.
14: *et* = *ed*.

SONNET 21

A seemingly simple opening, where Pico's feelings do not agree with his words, raises the complicated question of his poetry's relation to his poetic ability to express his experience. Is his poetry an incomplete mimesis of his love experience or is it an inadequate expression of how he feels? Later in the sonnet, line 8, do *Amor's* arrows inspire Pico to love or to write about his experience of love? Is his inability such that his writing turns gold into lead, his prayers "more inert and dumb than stone"?

We might also ask: in the sense of Dante's four levels of meaning, are his poems literal, allegorical, moral or anagogic—with the latter meaning to give a spiritual or mystical sense to his verse? The latter may not be so far off, because each *Amor* and *Madonna* have torn him between the ideal and corporeal.

1: Ïo = Io, with a dieresis over the *I* in order to make this dipthong count as two syllables, not as the normal one syllable so that the line has the usual eleven syllables common to Italian poetry.
2: *ca* = *che*.
3: *intrar* = *entrare*.
4: *eservi* = *esservi*.

5: *puoco* = *poco*.
6: *fia* = *sara*, antiquated future form of *essere*; *alaccia* = *allaccia*.
8: *reponga* = *ripone*, third person singular of *riporre*, *to replace*, but in the sense of a bow and arrow, translated as *to aim*.

9: *se muti* = *si muti*.
11: *sera* = usually *evening*, but also meaning *later*.

12: *oprar* = *oprare*, means *to work*, but the sense in English with a direct object *balance*—here, *bilanzi* = *bilancio*— could be *reach*, *achieve*, etc.
13: *como* = *come*; *se* = *si*.
14: *fiorí*, third person of the *passato remoto*, serving as a simple literary past tense.

SONNET 22

1-4: Pico expresses the intense emotions of love's trap as a man on opium feeling extreme cold, as if freezing in a fire, exploding.

1: *el = il*.
2: *lo freddo = il freddo*, probably as *lo* to increase the alliteration of the *o* sound.
3: *a lo = allo*.
4: *agiacciando = aggiacciando*.

5-8: Pico is sick with love once again, unable to escape, rendered awkward, mesmerized by her eyes.
5: *el mal = il male*.
8: *mei = miei*.

9-11: Love as a plague comes in a new guise, exciting him more.

12-14: He is bound by blond tresses in Love's lasting plot.
12: *a lacio = con un lacio*; *capei = capelli*.
13: *in la = nella*.
14: *vechieza = vecchiezza*; *el nostro = il nostro*, but here the sense is *il mio*.

SONNET 23

1-4: Pico asks if *Amor* is winged as in the paintings; i.e., fast and agile, why does he possess Pico to make him slow down to stillness? Then, if he is a child as Cupid, why does he torment the man he just defeated?
1: *alato = winged*, from *ala = wing*; *el è depincto = egli è dipinto*.
3: *piciol = picciolo = small*.
4: *vincto = vinto*.

5-8: If *Amor* wears a blindfold, how does he have such accurate glances striking a heart that is almost consummed to death?
5: *ochi = occhi*; *avincto = avvinto*.
6: *sí = cosí*.
7: *aflicto = afflitto*.
8: *vegio = veggo = vedo*.

9-11: Why is *Amor* full of contradictions?
10: *gli = egli*.
11: *et = ed*; *sí = cosí*.

12-14: Pico addresses the historic figure Francesco da Barberino (c. 1264–1348),

author of Trecento treatises on manners and love, as the pride of the Acidulous game of Venus and the only one in the Apollonian dance, wantng to know why all this is happening to him.
12: *Dimel* = *dimmi*.
13: *l'acidalio ludo* = the bitter game, but also a reference to the fountain Acidalia in Boeotia where Venus and the Graces bathed. Also, after she bathes there, it becomes Venus' surname.
14: *l'apollineo ballo* = *the Apollonian dance*, perhaps, according to Dilemmi, from Virgil's *Ecclogues*: vi:66: *Phoebi chorus*.

SONNET 24

1-8: A *copia* of examples of large amounts of various things to reinforce the great number of cares or pains in a lover's heart.

1: *Aeti* = Mount Athos in Greece, according to Dilemmi, in possible reference to Ovid's *Ars amandi*, II: 19, *tot sunt in amore dolores* = so many are suffering in love.

Also, from Greek mythology, after the Olympian dieties defeated the *Titans*, in anger *Gaia* raised up the *Giants* (*Gigantes*), one of whom, *Athos*, was vanguished by *Poseidon*. Hence, *Athos* represents, as do the *Titans*, irrational beings ruled by emotion, reinforcing Pico's theme of *Amor* causing *Reason* to flee. See other references to *Reason* in Sonnets 5, 7, 17, 28 and 41.
1: *lepor* = a Latinism for the Italian *lepori*.
2: *Como* = *come*; *son* = *sono*; *uom* = *uomo*.
3: *el* = *egli*, here translated in the impersonal as *one*.
3: *vago seno*, with *seno* literally as *bosom*, but the sense in the Petrarchan idiom is almost always as *heart*. Even though *vago* can mean rambling or undefined—or attractive or "of a lover," since the poem is of things that are missing, perhaps the best sense derives from *undefined* as *elusive*.
4: *iudicar* = obsolete for *giudicare*.
5: *monte Atlante* = Mount Atlas, a possible reference to *Atlas*, the *Titan* who was to forever hold up the heavens.
7: *el mar* = *il mare*; *stel'el ciel sereno* = *stelle nel cielo sereno*.
8: *cor* = *cuore*.

9-11: Many "pains, gasping and troubles…"
9: *son li martiri* = *sono i martiri*.

NOTES ON PICO'S SONNETS 97

10: *versan* = *versano*.
11: *'l* = *lo*.

12-14: As long as there is a little pleasure in loving, one does not notice the pain.
12: *cun puoco dolce tempre* = *con poco dolce tempere*.
13: *venen* = *veneno*; *om* = *uomo*.
14: *fin che* = *finché*; *capo cano* = literally, *grey-haired head*, but the sense is more immediate translated as *grizzled face*.

SONNET 25

A sonnet of loose sentences about the necessity of protecting one's soul no matter how much one must *go to her*, how much the body is ravaged.

2: *el* = *il*.
3: *el cel* = *il cielo*.
4: *om, dimi* = *uomo, dimmi*; *speme* = poetical for *hope*.

5: *tôrre* = a *syncope* or shortening of *togliere*.
6: *cor* = *cori*.
7: *passarem* = *passaremo*; *et* = *ed*.

9: *tal* = *tale*.
12: *oprar* = *operare*; *dèi* = *devi*.
13: *seco ne porti* = literally, *she carries it with her*, but the sense is *she carries it away*, so translated here *as she gets*, but the other way works, too.

SONNET 26

1-9: A compound dependent clause followed directly by a main clause, which, if simplified, would read, "If my lowly words ... may deserve ... that ornate and humble name, I don't want you to guide me."
1: dir di mei sospir = *dire di miei sospire*.
2: *ne la età mia aprile* = *nella età di mia aprile*, with *aprile* signifying springtime or, here, *youth*; i.e., *when I was young*.
3: vulgo = *volgo* = *mob, vulgar people*.
4: *tra'* = *trarre*; *imo* = *low*, as in *inferior* or *vile*.

8: *el* = *il*.

9: *vo'* = *voglio*; *di Latona il fio* = *il figlio di Latona* = Apollo.
10: *aganippei* = *Aganippis*, a possible reference to the source of inspiration, the Hippocrene spring on Mt. Helicon.
11: *Callïopè, Euterpe o Clio* = three of the nine Muses, specifically of eloquence, music and history, although these three have the attribute of poetry, as well.

12-14: Pico laments no muse supports him.
12: *ciel* = *cielo*.

SONNET 27

A clear and direct poem of loose sentences. God, the *Factore* of line 5, created Pico's lady to bring honor to the world and set off war within him, although his spirit glories in her presence, of which he will write for the ages.

4: inferïore, with a dieresis over the second *I* to make the dipthong *io* into two syllables.

11: *dil* = *del*.

14: *texendo* = there is no equivalent Italian word. If there were, it would be the verb *testere*. However, there is a root in Italian, *testo* = text, and derivations, *tesstore* and *tessitore*, meaning author. Texendo is a gerund, another of Pico's Latinisms, here from the Latin verb *texere, to weave, braid or construct*, referring to Pico's act of writing these sonnets. In the first person, this gives this poem and these sonnets an immediacy for both Pico and the reader.
14: *istoria* = *storia*.

SONNET 28

1-4: Pico addresses those who are in love by explaining that a thousand times *Amor* has put him, as predicted by the Tarot, in their ranks.

1: *ben* = *bene*; *cun* = *con*.
2: *uom sagio* = *uomo saggio*.
3: *ne la* = *nella*.
4: *che empieti de triunfi soi le carte* = *che empiti i suoi trionfi delle carte*. Latinate, a hyperbaton, not a normal word order, common in Latin, but not to this extent

in Italian—and, also an elliptical phrase which reads *which completed his triumphs* [predicted by] *the Tarot*.

Empire = *to fill* or *complete*, with *empiti* that past plural participle, but the sense here is completed his triumphs of the Tarot.
4: *le carte* = *the Tarot*.

5-8: *Amor* shows him that level or true heaven that confuses his heart.
5: *ragion* = *ragione* = see notes on *reason* in Sonnets 5, 7, 17, 24, 28 and 41.
6: *dil cel* = *del cielo*.
7: *cun* = *con*.
8: *'l cor voria partir* = *il cuore vorrebbe partire*.

9-11: Fortune makes the souls of lovers neither happy nor sad, with thoughts fighting one another.
9: *ancor* = *ancora*; *gioir* = *gioire*.
9-10: *Onde ancor né gioir nostra alma o trista/far può Fortuna...* = *Onde ancora Fortuna può fare nostra alma / né gioir o trista...* = placing the subject last in this phrase for emphasis.
10: *furno* = *furono*.
11: *ochi* = *occhi*; *lor* = *loro*.

Jealousy, who always follows their lord *Amor*, offers such a view to Pico's heart which then feared his lady.
12: *'l* = *il*.
13: *seguir suol* = *seguire solo*; *coltal* = *cotale*.
14: *cor* = *cuore*; *alor* = *alora*.

SONNET 29

Pico's own inner struggles with the love and passion he feels takes a serious social turn when he is led to a cliff and then begs for pardon, whence he is changed and pulls a new fruit from his eternal torment.
1: *el* = *il*.
3: *mi celò* = *celai*, first person *passato remoto*.
4: *ir* = *ire*.

7: *perdon* = *perdono*.

8: *l'uom* = *l'uomo*.

9: *Et* = *Ed*; *exempio* = *esempio*; *popul* = *popolo*.
10: *cun lor* = *con loro*.
11: *commun* = *comune*.

12: *fin* = *fine*.
13: *Perdon* = *Perdono*, but the sense here is to the community, *perdonatemi*.

SONNET 30

Pico tells his spirit not to tell the Maker it will not be with him in heaven because it is corrupted. But, alas, Pico says the Maker likes to put his spirit with Pico so that they can be with him in the kingdom.

2: *piè* = *piede*.
4: *el* = *il*; *cal* = *calo*.

5: *fei* = *feci*; *et or* = *ed ora*.
6: *et* = *ed*.
8: *el* = *il*.

11: *però parte nel ciel non avrai meco* = *però non avrai parte con me nel ciel* = another Latinate phrase, a hyperbaton, a jumbled word order to us, but thinking in Latin, a phrasing that both fits the rhyme scheme but also emphasizes he does not want his spirit with him by concluding with *meco*.

13-14: *Hence, while he likes to cover you/with my veil* = Pico speaks to his spirit about *the Maker covering it with his veil*—a Neoplatonic refernence to one's spirit in the material body.
13: *vel* = *velo*; *seco* = *con lui*.
14: *possàn* = *possiamo*.

SONNET 31

Pico asks *Amor* why he draws his friends and him into the game of love. He is neither less satisfied than weak, nor does he fear serving *Amor*.
2: *trarmi* = *trarre me*; *gioco* = *giuoco*.

3-4: *Del vanegiar non men sazio che fioco/già son* = *io sono già non meno sazio che fioco dal vaneggiare* = another hyperbaton.

Pico knows how quickly happiness vanishes, how earthly pleasure lasts only a little, and how every dead man is stripped of his body.
5: *amorzi* = *smorzi*.
6: *foco* = *fuoco*.
7: *piacer terren* = *piacere terreno*; *puoco* = *poco*.
8: *uom* = *uomo*.
8: *come ogni uom morte di sua spoglia scorzi* = how every dead man is stripped of his shell = a Neoplatonic reference to the immaterial soul in the material boduy.

Those who follow *Amor* and entrap a cripple are exhausted without prey.
9: *stroppio* = *storpio* = cripple.
10: *a' lacci* = *ai lacci*.
11: *exinanita* = Latin root *exinanio* = *to strip*, *to empty*, turned into an Italian past participle with the *ita.* used as an adjective.

Pico remembers the explosion and incurable wound of love, but he has cured himself and is now fresh.
12: *che rimembrandol scoppio* = *che rimembrandoci scoppio*.
13: *fata insanabil* = *fatta insanabile*.

SONNET 32

If Pico's lord—God or *Amor*—has chosen him for heaven, he asks to be free of predestination.
1: *ellecto* = *eletto*; *cel* = *cielo*.
2: *Segnor* = *Signore*; *fa'* = *fate*.
4: *cel* = *cielo*; *de* = *di*.

Death reigns over lovers because people give in to bodily pleasures. In the Neoplatonic sense, the body, mortal matter, dominates the soul, immaterial and eternal.
6: *el dí* = *il giorno* = *iusto* = *giusto*.
6: …*come el dí sette volte el iusto cada…* = a refernce to Old Testament Proverbs 24:16: *For though the righteous fall **seven** times, they rise again, but the wicked stumble...* In Italian: *Perché se il giusto cade sette volte, egli si rialza, ma gli empi soccombono nella sventura…*

7: *agrada* = *aggrada*.
8: *son fral* = *sono frale* or *fragile*.

9: Either God or *Amor*—it is unclear—made Pico.
9: *su la* = *sulla*.
10. *mirabil* = *mirabile*.

Pico's heart burns with the faith of love, but asks for *Amor's* guidance if he wanders off the proper path.
12: *donque* = *dunque*; *fé* = *fede*. On faith, see note on *Sonnet 13*, line 12.
13: *s'i' vo fuor* = *se io vado fuori*.
14: *pastor* = *pastore*.

SONNET 33

In this poem, we see the Neoplatonic struggle of the pure, immaterial soul (*nudata d'ogni vizio*) trapped in a material and mortal body that is dominated by worldly passions (*chi furar volse la febëa lampa*). *Stealing the Apollonian lamp* is impure.

From the time God created his pure soul free of vice, Pico had a forgone fate as he became a poet as he wanted to steal the Apollonian lamp.
1: *dil celo* = *del cielo*.
3: *a'* = *ai*; *pors'inizio* = *porso inizio* = *a given beginning*, but in this poetical sense, *fated beginning* is better.
4: *febëa*, a dieresis over the *e* to add an extra syllable of the word *febea* = poetical, taken from *Phoebus* = *Apollo*.

Pico's lady, whom one cannot escape, descended from heaven.
5: *uom* = *uomo*.

This lady takes everything except your name.
10: *irreparabil* = *irreparabile*.
11: *deprecar* = *deprecare*; *cun* = *con*.
This lady shows Pico he must obey his senses; i.e., his passion.
12: *ne gli ochi* = *negli occhi*.
14: *oberdir* = *obedire*; *commandar* = *commandare*.

SONNET 34

At the beginning, Pico did not think he would struggle between the moral (or honest) choices and the overwhelming (enormous) feelings he would have.
2: *Principio* = *Beginning*.
3: *l'onesto, lo enorme* = *l'onetso e lo enorme*, literally, *the honest, the enormous*, but in the sense of the emotions and Pico's sense here, *the moral and the overwhelming*.
4: *cun* = *con*.

When a man believes he is advancing, the sun sets and he sleeps, becoming arid so he can no longer recognize beauty.
5: *l'uom crede el gli avanzi* = *l'uomo crede che elgli avanzi*.
6: *el* = *il*.

His lady did not notice him on his journey in exile.
10-11: *esser* = *essere*, here as *anaphora*, repeating a word at the beginning of each phrase.

While Pico must think less of his mistakes, he keeps Charity, Faith and Hope in his heart.
12: *e' mie' passati error* = *i miei passati errori*.
12-13: *mentre e' mie' passati error pensando/men vo* = *mentre devo pensare meno sui miei errori*.
14: *de Carità, di Fede e di Speranza* = *of Faith, Hope and Charity* = the three theological virtues.

SONNET 35

Under terrestrial light in a temporal world, earthly fortune changes the good with the bad.
2: *el sol* = *il sole*.
3: *a le terrestre luce* = *alle terrestre luci*.
4: *el ben col male varia fortune parte* = *fortuna varia il bene (parte) con il male parte* = a hyperbaton that emphasizes fortune rules one's life.
What offends Pico is that the light above him is never clear, he always cries and even more so through the night ...
6: *vien* = *viene*.
7: *Verson lacrime sempre le mie luce* = literally, *they pour tears always my lights*, but

le mie luce is a metaphor here for Pico's *eyes*.
8 *'l sol* = *il sole*.

… and no less when the sun rises, while dread condenses in some book.
9: *men* = *meno*.
10: *el sudor* = *il sudore*.

Pico wants his trip to *Inferno* to be in darkness being a dried book in flames, with his poetry as the only light in this terrestrial world.
14: *exsicato* = *essicato*, with the Latin verb being *exsiccare*.

SONNET 36

Pico's relationship is consummated, but not emotionally easily.

Pico's woman was pensive, sad, empty of joy and loaded with pain as *Amore* spoke with her at midnight, when her crying awoke him.
1: *mesta* = apocopated form of *mestato*, from the verb *mestare* = to stir, blend or mingle, but here, the sense is *agitated*.
2: *vòta* = *vuota*; *carca* = antiquated form of *carcata* or *caricata*.
3: *cun* = *con*.
4: *meza nocte* = *mezzanotte*.

Amor appeared to her nude, in the guise of a messenger. He explains that his heart would forgive the mistake if it would stop.
5: *ignudo* = *nudo*; *vesta* = colloquial version of *veste*
6: *de un mesaggio* = *di un messagio*; *el* = *il*.
8: *s'aresta* = *s'arresta*.

She asked for pity from who would not forgive.
9: *Ella a pietà non ch'a perdon si volse* = an elliptical hyerbaton, literally, *She to pity not who would to pardon turn*. Poetically in English, the following might work, but sound antiquated: *She to pity who would not turn to pardon*. The meaning, though, is *She asked for pity from who would not pardon*.
10: *ché* = *perché*.
11: *el cor* = *il cuore*; *i strale* = *gli strali*, changed to *strale* fit the rhyme scheme.

His flames and arrows drawn into her moist womb, with cruel *Amore* beside her

uttering, "He has flown here with my wings."
12: *ne l'umido* = *nell'umido*; *alor* = *allora*; *racolse* = *raccolse*.
13: *empio* = *impious* or *inhuman*, here, the sense seemed *cruel*, given the events as they have transpired.

SONNET 37

Interesting that in the previous sonnet, after he consumates his physical relationship with his *woman*, Pico now in this sonnet laments the state of Italy, which may express what transpired after he tried to away with his love Margherita, the wife of Giuliano Mariotto de' Medici, one of Lorenzo de' Medici's cousins, while he was in Arezzo. In particular, the last line is telling, for Pico was beaten, broken physically and psychologically, and then imprisoned.

Italy is dark, her splendor in other places, having left.
1: *como* = *come*; *umbra* = *ombra*.
2: *parte* = *parti*, left in the singular to fit the rhyme.
3: *riman* = *rimane*.
4: *el tuo vivo splendor ch'altrove or luce* = *il tuo vivo splendore che altrove [è] ora luce*, another elliptical phrase.

Italy's light gives life, but has departed.
5: *De' soi bei raggi aviva le tue luce* = *Dei suoi bei raggi avviva le tue luci*, with the plural *luci* changed to the singlular *luce* to fit the rhyme.
6: *a'* = *ai*.
The dark lights appear to Pico as spirits of Dis, the lower circles of hell.
9: *Alor me parerai como* = *Allora mi parerai come*.
10: *stano* = *stanno*.

If Pico cries with Italy, he will say, "I am no longer who I was."
12: *fie cognosciuto* = *sarà conosciuto*.
13: *avia* = *avvia*; *teco* = *con te*.
14: *Io non son più quella ch'i' fui* = *Io non sono più quella che io fui*.

SONNET 38

Pico gives several reasons to a friend about how he was taken in by love, for which he was almost killed. *Amor*'s arrow rests in his eye, a particularly visceral image wrought with a genuine pain more severe than the pain his lady ever caused. With *Amor*'s arrow in his eye, perhaps a metaphor for his lady's beauty, at this point, though, it is a grotesque one, directly implying blindness, disfigurement and pain. He then explains to his friend to have faith in his suffering or else he won't survive—perhaps they both will not.

Before these events, his was a struggle with *Amore*, but it is different now. He is being punished, which hurts him, but more importantly, makes him sad. For Pico, a man of such monumental talent and ability, this is failure, full and complete.

1: *Per ...* = This begins a seven line *anaphora*, using the preposition *per* repetitively at the beginning of each phrase.
1: *ochi* = *occhi*; *avinto* = *avvinto*.
2: *ne l'acque* = *nell'acque*.
3: *pel* = *per il*.

6: *pel strale a cui el mio cor* = *per il strale a cui il mio core*.
7: *de cui mal* = *di cui male*.
8: *ch'indi ne fui poi quasi extinto* = *quindi* (or, *da lì*) *io fui quasi estinto da tutto quello*.

9: *stral* = *strale*; *ocio* = *occhio*.
11: *adumbra* = *oscura, ombra*.

12: *díe fede* = *dia fede* = *abbia fede*.
13: *no 'l* = *non il*.

SONNET 39

Suffering, nonetheless, we have Pico's beautiful and clear profession of faith in love which he equates with every good thing, each and all gifts from almighty Jove. A sonnet beautiful in its clarity and simplicity.

SONNET 40

Pico recounts to his Lord where his heart was first bound, where his pain began and where *Amor* did to him what he wanted. Pico would do this, but not if she scorns them.

NOTES ON PICO'S SONNETS   107

1: *Segnor* = *Signore*.
2: *ligato fu el mio core* = *fu legato il mio cuore*.
2-3: *ove … ove …* = an *anaphora*, the repetition of *ove* at the beginning of each phrase.
3: *ove el mio pianto comenciò e 'l dolore* = *dove il mio pianto ed il mio dolore cominciarono*.
4: *fece Amor di me quel che a lui parve* = *Amor fece di me quel che* [pare] *a lui parvo* = an elliptical phrase.

Apollo enters and tells Pico to sing of a clear splendor and leave Amor who they always flatter with false illusions.
5: Here enters, not *Amore*, but *Apollo*.

Pico would do this, but not if she scorns them.
10: *facto emulo a nui* = *fatto di noi emuli* = *emuli* is a false friend, not *emulations*, but rather, *rivals* or *competitors*.
11: *men* = *meno*.

Pico says he conditionally would obey Apollo.
12: *et* = *ed*.
13: *te* = *ti*.
14: *un stil* = *uno stile*.

SONNET 41

Pico feels changed from what he was before, changed by a noble plague as Amor took the keys to his heart and gave them to his enemy, his lady, who accepted them and then bound him to servitude, after which jealousy guided him through depraved streets. As such, reason left him, with new thoughts and wants coming in to him. With all this, from his lady's prison, he saw his soul leave.

1: *me* = *mi*; *en* = *in*.
3: *cor* = *core*; *tôrme* = *togliere da me*.
4: *porle* = *porre le*; *man* = *mano*.

6-7: *d'una servitú legera e grave/legarme* = *legarmi d'una servitú legera e grave*.

9: Ragion = see extended the comments on *reason* in *Sonnet 17*.
11: *alogiar* = *alloggiare*; *con meco* = *con me*.

14: *inanti* = *innanzi*.

SONNET 42

Dilemmi's interpretation of *Pa* and *Po*, are *Pa* as the lady, possibly *Pleona* from *Carmina 14* and, from scholastic terminology, *Pa(tiens)* = from the Latin *patior* = *to suffer, wait, experience*. While *Po* as the *Po(eta)* and, again from scholastic terminology, *Po(tens)* = Latin for *able, potent, strong*; i.e., *capable of action*. We should comment that, in this sense, then, we see the contrasting *vita contemplativa* and *vita activa*, but should keep in mind that in Pico's scheme, the lady is anything but passive. Moreover, this dialogue is not one sided, but a give-and-take on equal footing, which discounts the implied essences of each charactonym.

1: *el cor* = *il core*; *truova* = *trova*.
2: *foco* = *fuoco*.
3: *acti* = *atti*.
4: *ochi* = *occhi*; *mova* = *muove*.

5: *el* = *il*; *anze 'l rinova* = *anzi il rinnova*.
7: *nascon* = *nascono*.
8: *stil* = *stile*; *unde* = *onde*.

11: *agiaccia* = *agghiaccia*.
12: *legiadre* = *leggiadre*.

13: *Donque* = *Dunque*; *me vedi* = *mi vedi*.
14: *Ben* = *Bene*; *però che* = *perocché* = *perché*.
15: *agiacciando* = *agghiacciando*.

SONNET 43

It was springtime when Pico arrived at an inn where nature ruled, but the sense here is that he arrived at the edge.
1: *ne la* = *nella*; *el sol* = *il sole*.
1: *la stagione* = springtime.
2: *a' dui* = *ai due*; *offizio* = *officio*, translated here as *sacrament*, but *offering* would work just as well.
2: *due figli di Leda* = Apollo and Artemis.

3: *ch'io gionsi a l'umbra d'un ospizio* = *che io giunsi all'ombra di un ospizio*.
4: *süe* = a *dieresis* over the *e* to separate it from the dipthong *ue* in order to make two syllables, not one; *extende* = *estende*.

There a nymph of great beauty descended from the sky.
5: *pedaglion* = *padiglioni*; *trabacche* = *travacche*.
6: *gionse da l'alto ciel* = *giunse dall'alto cielo*.

Apollo, Jove and all the other gods were there to violate her, but Cupid with Phoebus worked with her to defeat their plans.
11: *cun* = *con*; *triunfarne* = *trionfarli*.

Incensed, Jove ascended in his chariot to get revenge, but Pico's friend (either Cupid or Phoebus) saw Jove and fled with the nymph.
12: *el car* = *il carro*.
13: *l'acorto amico e fido* = *l'accorto e fido amico*.
14: *s'ascose in vista, e se 'n fugí cun lei* = *si nascose alla vista e sene fuggi con lei*.

SONNET 44

Time passes, but Apollo is eternal. A silver-winged doe of his appears to Pico.
1: *l'or' distingue* = *l'ora (o il tempo) decide*.
2: *soi corser* = *suoi corsari* = *suoi cavalli (di Apollo)*.
4: *Cerva che avea d'argento i vanni* = *Cerva che aveva i vanni d'argento*, a deer is an attribute of Apollo.

Two hunters follow her, with one enticing her with an apple.
5: *Doi cacciator ch'avevan squarzati i panni* = *Due cacciatori che avevano squarciati i panni*.
6: *sequivan* = *sequivanno*; *glie* = *la*.
7: *el mele* = *la mela*.

The doe, innocent, approached the trap.
9: *L'animaletto* = *L'animale innocente*.
10: *dubio* = *dubbio*.
10-11: *... e pur al mele/che piú la se acostasse a me alor parve* = *nondimeno, la cerva se accosta la mela, dunque a me, sembra una bambina*.

As Pico bitterly fretted over this state of affairs, the doe vanished.
12: *Et io de ciò* = *Ed io di ciò*.
13: *me acorgea* = *m'accorgeva*. Dropping the *v* in imperfect endings was done in both poetry and prose.

SONNET 45

Although in Sonnet 44 with Pico's personal cathartic experience of *innocence* escaping the predatory aspect of human evil, he concludes his sonnet sequence with a roaring indictment of the state of affairs in Italy as unprincipled predatory states wreak havoc on each other and their citizenry. If *Amor* is difficult between lovers and friends, that distance is multiplied at the level of state-on-state violence throught the peninsula, a vast expansion of Pico's metaphors of human relations into a grand social statement. We might say that reaching these conclusions as a young man just in his early 30s—a young man advocating for many theological changes—he was murdered through arsenic poisoning.

Gone from the potential of amorous love to the hardcore reality of his time in this sequence.

2: *Il Papa* = *Innocenzo VIII* (1443-92); *iace* = *giace*.
3: *Marzoco a palla gioca* = Florence under Medici rule, with *Marzocco* the lion as the symbol of the *commune* and the balls as part of the Medici coat of arms.
4: *la Bissa è pregna* = Milano under the Visconti, with the *Biscione* or viper either eating or giving birth to a man as its coat of arms. *Pregna* = literally pregnant or symbolically, full of venom.
5: *Ferrando* = *Ferdinando I d'Aragona*, King of Napoli (1431- 94), with *el scorno* (*lo scorno*) being the *Congiura dei Baroni* (Revolt of the Barons, 1485-86).
6: *San Marco* = Venezia.
7: *la vincta Bissa ora San Georgio offende* = *Milano* reconquers *Genoa* in 1488.
8: *la Lupa a scampo* = escaped *Siena* with its emblem of the wolf, eternally vigilant having escaped Florentine control.

9: *Sega la grassa stracia in Mal avezi* = the rulers of *Bologna*, the Bentivolgio family, whose symbol was a *saw*, dealt with the republican Malvezzi family with cruelty in 1488. *Stracia* = *strazia*; *avezi* = *avvezzi* = accustomed, usual.
10: *la Pantiera circondata crida* = the Panther symbolizes *Lucca*, here surrounded and shreiking (or crying). *crida* = *grida*.

11: *femine e puti tien Romagna in pezi* = *Romagna (Bologna) tiene in pezzi femine e bambini*, which describes a particularly brutal massacre of women and children in *Faenza* in 1488.

12: *Da Aquile e Griffi al ciel ne va le strida* = *Aquille e griffi vanno stridando nel cielo*, with eagles and griffins symbolizing other cities in general, each screaming in pain and suffering.

13: *e 'l ciel non ode* = *e il cielo non ode*, the heavens do not hear the suffering, so no relief from anywhere or anyone. Thus, reigns on the *status quo*, as do the Egyptian Moors and as did Tarquin, Sardanapalus, Midas and Crassus, each a tyrant in antiquity.

Endnotes

1   Jacques Derrida, *Of Grammatology*, trans. Gayatri Chakravorty Spivak, (Baltimore: John Hopkins University Press, 1976), 92-93.

2   For the original texts of the *Certame coronari*, see *De vera amicitia. I testi del primo certame coronario* di L. Bertolini (Modena: Pannini, 1993). For a quick reference, see the *Treccani* article, *Certame coronario*; and also "Selections from the *Certame coronario*" in Marc A. Cirigliano, *Melancolia Poetica* (Leicester, UK: Troubador Publishing Ltd.), 2007, 175-189.

3   In clarifying how to read Italian Renaissance documents contextually, Ugo Procacci cites this statement by Alberti on the rising status of painting as a liberal art: "Leon Battista Alberti scriveva - per la pittura circa il 1430, appunto agli inizi del rinascimento: "Noi però ci reputeremo ad voluptà primi avere presa questa palma, d'avere ardito commendare alle lettere questa arte la pittura appunto sottilissima e nobilissima." See his "L'uso dei documenti negli studi di storia dell'arte e le vicende politiche ed economiche in Firenze durante il primo Quattrocento nel loro rapporto con gli artisti," *Donatello e il suo tempo, Atti Dell'VIII Convegno Internazionale di Studi sul Rinascimento* (Firenza-Padova: Istituto nazionale di studi sul rinascimento, 1966), 23. On this topic, see also, Dr. John M. Hunt, "The status of the artist in renaissance Italy," in *Smarthistory*, May 14, 2023. Accessed June 1, 2023, https://smarthistory.org/the-status-of-the-artist-in-renaissance-italy/.

       A sound introduction to the Italian Renaissance is found in: Peter Burke, *The Italian Renaissance: Culture and Society in Italy*, 3rd edition, (Princeton: Princeton University Press 2014) and Ingrid D. Rowland, *From Heaven to Arcadia: The Sacred and the Profane in the Renaissance* (New York: NYREV, 2005). Suggested are also, Alison Cole, *Italian Renaissance Courts: Art, Pleasure and Power* (London: Laurence King Publishing, 2016) and Christopher S. Celenza, *The Intellectual World of the Italian Renaissance* (New York: Cambridge University Press, 2018). Older but still viable is Giulio Carlo Argan, *Storia dell'arte italiana*, vols. 2 & 3, (Firenze: Sansoni, 1981).

4   The original text reads: "Nè sia però nessuno che questa toscana lingua come poco ornata e copiosa disprezzi. Imperocchè, se bene e giustamente le sue ricchezze ed

ornamenti saranno estimati, non povera questa lingua, non rozza, ma abbondante e pulitissima sarà riputata. Nessuna cosa gentile, florida, leggiadra, ornata, nessuna acuta, distinta, ingegnosa, sottile, nessuna ampia e copiosa, nessuna alta, magnifica, sonora, nessuna altra finalmente ardente, animosa, concitata, si puote imaginare; della quale non pure in quelli duo primi Dante e Petrarca, ma in questi altri ancora i quali tu, signore, hai suscitati, i chiarissimi esempi non risplendano. Fu l'uso della rima (secondo che in una latina epistola scrive il Petrarca) ancora appresso gli antichi Romani assai celebrato. Il quale, per molto tempo intermesso, cominciò poi nella Sicilia non molti secoli avanti a rifiorire; e di qui per la Francia sparto, finalmente in Italia, quasi in un suo ostello, è pervenuto." From Alessandro D'Ancona and Orazio Bacci, eds., *Manuale della Letterature Italiana*, v. 2, (Florence: G. Barbèra, 1929), 176.

5   The matter of the long-standing success of Lorenzo de' Medici's campaign to make Tuscan on par with Latin and then up until today the dominant dialect among all the *volgari* of Italy is discussed in detail by Ingeborg Walter in her *Lorenzo Magnifico e il suo tempo*, trans. Roberto Zapperi, (Roma: Donzelli, 2005), 245-48.

6   Lorenzo's text is easily found online through WikiSource: Lorenzo de' Medici, "Comento del magnifico Lorenzo de' Medici sopra alcuni de' suoi sonetti," *Opere*, v. 2, ed. by Attilio Simioni, (Bari: Laterza, 1914). Accessed Nov. 11, 2022, BEIC, https://it.m.wikisource.org/wiki/Opere_(Lorenzo_de%27_Medici)/II._Comento_del_magnifico_Lorenzo_de%27_Medici_sopra_alcuni_de%27_suoi_sonetti.

For Lorenzo's own poetry, see Lorenzo de' Medici. *Canzoniere*, ed. by Paolo Orvieto, (Milano: Mondadori), 1984.

7   Cirigliano, *Poetica*, 32-33.

8   Tullio De Mauro makes the point that Dante's language becomes the language of modern Italy when he writes, "Se guardiamo ai discorsi e testi italiani (e l'analogo avviene in ogni lingua), ci avvediamo che essi sono letteralmente intessuti delle circa duemila parole del vocabolario fondamentale, in cui le altre decine di migliaia si incastonano. Dotti e indotti convergono in ciò, e più precisa- mente le parole del vocabolario fondamentale di una lingua occupano, in media, il 92 o 93% di tutte le parole che figurano nei testi e discorsi.

"Questo nocciolo funzionale del nostro apparato lessicale è anche la parte più antica. Quando Dante comincia a scrivere la Commedia il vocabolario fondamentale è già costituito al 60%. La Commedia lo fa proprio, lo integra e col suo sigillo lo trasmette nei secoli fino a noi. Alla fine del Trecento il vocabolario fondamentale italiano è configurato e completo al 90%. Ben poco è stato aggiunto dai secoli seguenti. Tutte le volte che ci è dato di parlare con le sue parole, e accade quando riu- sciamo a essere assai chiari, non è enfasi retorica dire che parliamo la lingua di Dante. È un fatto." See, Tullio De Mauro, *Grande dizionario italiano dell'uso*, (Torino, UTET, 1999), 1166.

9   Cirigliano, *Poetica*, 100-101.
10 *The New Life of Dante Alighieri*, trans. by Charles Eliot Norton, (New York: Houghton Mifflin, 1896), 4.

ENDNOTES   **115**

11   *New Life*, 6.
12   Mario Pomilio emphasizes the interiority of Petrarch's *Rerum vulgarium fragmenta*, "All of Petrarch's varied and complex speculation is nothing more than an invitation and a call to interiority. The "noli foras ire; in te redi: in interno homine habitat veritas" [do not go outside; comeback to yourself: in the inner man lives truth, *Soliloqui agostiniani*, I, 2, 7] is a principle from which Petrarch at no time wanted to depart from and which conditions his entire work and undoubtedly gives meaning to that assiduous and thoughtful search for himself which certainly constitutes the most revolutionary aspect of his Poems." See Mario Pomilio. *Petrarca e l'idea di poesia: Una monografia inedita*, ed. by Cecilia Gibellini, (Rome: Studium, 2016), Kindle, 1467.
13   Musa, Mark. *Petrarch Canzoniere* (Bloomington: Indiana University Press, 1999), Kindle, 1-2.
14   Musa, *Canzoniere*, 1-2.
15   Musa, *Canzoniere*, 55-56.
16   Francesco Petrarch , "On the Nature of Poetry To his Brother Gherardo," *Familiar Letters*, from James Harvey Robinson, ed. and trans., *Petrarch: The First Modern Scholar and Man of Letters* (New York: G.P. Putnam, 1898), part of the *Hanover Historical Texts Project*,1995, 261-275, accessed Feb. 2, 2023, https://history.hanover.edu/texts/petrarch/pet13.html.
17   Petrarch, "Nature of Poetry."
18   Musa, *Canzoniere*, 441-442.
19   Musa, *Canzoniere*, 83-84.
20   Musa, *Canzoniere*, 203-204.
21   For a background on Pico's thought, see both Brian P. Copenhaver, *Magic and the Dignity of Man: Pico della Mirandola and His Oration in Modern Memory* (Cambridge, MA: Belknap Press of Harvard University Press, 2019) and Giolio Busi and Raphael Ebgi, *Giovanni Pico della Mirandola Mito, Magia, Qabbalah* (Torino: Einaudi, 2014).
22   "Legi, Laurenti Medice, rythmos tuos, quos tibi vernaculae Musae per aetatem teneram suggesserunt. Agnovi Musarum et Gratiarum legitimam faeturam; aetatis tenerae opus non agnovi. Quis enim in tuis rythmis et numerosa versuum iunctura saltantes ad numerum gratias non persenserit? Quis in canoro dicendi genere et modulato canentes Musas non audiat?," Giovanni Pico della Mirandola, *Lettere*, ed. by Francesco Borghesi, (Firenze: Olschki, 2018), 86-87.
23   "Sunt apud vos duo praecipue celebrati poetae Florentinae linguae, Franciscus Petrarcha et Dantes Aligerius, de quibus illud in universum sim praefatus, esse ex eruditis, qui res in Francisco, verba in Dante desiderent; in te qui mentem habeat et aures, neutrum desideraturum, in quo non sit videre, an res oratione, an verba sententiis magis illustrentur," Pico, *Lettere*, 87.
24   "*Rime sparse* is the Italian version of Petrarch's Latin title *Rerum vulgarium fragmenta*." Musa, *Canzoniere*, 520.
25   "Franciscus quidem si reviviscat quod attinet ad sensus quis dubitat ultro herbam

tibi daturum, adeo tu et acutus semper gravis et subtilis, ille vero de medio plurimum arripiens sententias colorat verbis, et quae sunt gregaria egregia facit genere dicendi, in quo videamus quid tibi ille, quid tu illi praestes, in quibusdam dulcior apparuerit. Sed mihi illius dulcedo, ut ita dixerim, dulciter acida et suaviter austera," Pico, *Lettere*, 87.

26 "… Franciscum quandoque non respondere pollicitis, habentem quod allectet in prima specie, sed ulterius non satisfaciat," Pico, *Lettere*, 89.

27 "Primas certe, quod ad stilum spectat, denegaturum tibi neminem puto, ita est Dantes nonnunquam horridus, asper et strigosus, ut multum rudis et impolitus, hoc eius etiam aurarii fatentur," Pico, *Lettere*, 88.

28 "Si de Deo, de anima, de beatis agitur, affert quae Thomas, quae Augustinus de his scripserunt, et fuit ille in his tractandis meditandisque tam frequens quam assiduus, tu in obeundis maximis negociis publicis octogenarius antistes, qui ut cumque caetera succedant, hoc tamen continue saxum volvit, ut alicunde pecuniam corrodat, quod vitium senibus cognatum et familiare semper fuit. Quid dicam de parasito nostro, qui a parcissimo sene coenam saliarem dissimulans extorquet, qui ipsum, ut ita dicam, singularissime pumicem emungit. Non fuit tam preclare in Dante hoc fecisse, quam non fecisse turpe fuerat," Pico, *Lettere*, 88-89.

29 George Steiner, *Real Presences* (Chicago: University of Chicago Press, 1989), 10-12.

30 "Quippe ego dum geminis (ut aiunt) sellis sedere volo, utraque excludor, sit que demum (ut dicam paucis) ut nec poëta, nec rhetor sim, ne que philosophus," Giovanni Pico della Mirandola, *Sonetti*, ed. by Giorgio Dilemmi, (Torino: Einaudi, 1994), v.

31 On these points, see S.A. Farmer, *Syncretism in the West: Pico's 900 Theses (1486)* (Tempe, AZ: Medieval and Renaissance Texts and Studies, 1998).

32 From Pico's letter to Andra Corneo: "Romam prope diem proficiscar, illic hyematurus, nisi vel repens casus, vel nova intercidens fortuna alio me traxerit. Inde fortasse audies, quid tuus Picus in vita umbratili et cellularia, contemplando profecerit: . . . Quod scribis de re uxoria, nec de nihilo dictum existimo …. Rythmos meos Hetruscos non est quod desideres, iamdudum amatoriis lutibus nuntium remisimus alia meditantes. Sed hoc te quoque monitum volo, Lauram tuam, si eam esses editurus, supprimas adhuc aliquot dies. Nam forsan paulo mox legent nostri homines de amore (vide quid dicam) quos nendum legerunt …" For information on Costanza's letter and Pico's letter to Andrea Corneo, see Commissione municipale di storia patria e di arti belle. *Memorie storiche della città e dell'antico ducato della Mirandola*. (Mirandola: Gaetano Cagarelli, 1876. *Internet Archive*, accessed June 3, 2023, https://archive.org/details/memoriestoriche01itagoog/page/n237/mode/2up?q=Arezzo.

33 Giovanni Pico Della Mirandola (nephew). *The Life of Pico della Mirandola*. Trans. by Thomas More, edited with introduction and notes by J. M. Rigg, with an introductory essay by Walter Pater, (London: David Nutt, 1890), 37. Published by the Ex-classics Project, 2011. https://www.exclassics.com/Pico/pico.pdf.

34 "… the younger Pico—who was at least as close to Savonarola as his uncle—

intervened to make the elder Pico's letters, as they appeared in the collected works that the nephew edited in 1496, underwrite the pious *Life* that introduces the whole collection.

"The Pico of that *Life* is a Savonarolan saint who came almost too late to salvation but finally rejected the world, the flesh and the devil. This is not the Pico who traveled to Rome a few years before to take on the whole world in a failed philosophical extravaganza; nor the Pico who bungled an attempt to carry off a married woman whose husband was named Medici—no less; nor the Pico with whom Ficino bantered about his missteps and misfortunes in letters loaded with astro-mythological allusions. It may be that the disasters of 1486–7 chastened the young nobleman enough to explain the muffling of Kabbalah in the *Heptaplus* and the jarring recantation that we find in the *Disputations*. But since the editor of the *Disputations*, Gianfrancesco Pico, also edited the letters that he selected to underwrite a tendentious *Life* of his uncle, and since Gianfrancesco himself was not just a devout fideist but also a prodigiously productive scholar and an original thinker, we should not dismiss the possibility that the *Disputations* ought to be read more as a pendant to the nephew's *Life* of Pico than as proof of penitence in a final phase of his uncle's meteoric career." Brian Copenhaver, "Giovanni Pico della Mirandola," *Stanford Encyclopedia of Philosophy*, accessed July 16, 2023, https://plato.stanford.edu/entries/pico-della-mirandola/.

35   Gianni Gallello, et al., "Poisoning histories in the Italian renaissance: The case of Pico Della Mirandola and Angelo Poliziano," *National Library of Medicine*, May 2018, accessed Feb. 3, 2023, https://pubmed.ncbi.nlm.nih.gov/29609050/.

36   There are a number of sources on Italian prosody, including an article "Metrica" in *Trecanni*. The examples of *dieresis* and *syneresis*, plus *dialeph* and *synalepha*, are from Costanzo Di Girolamo, *Manualetto di metrica italiana* (Rome: Carocci, 2021), 23-25. An older classic that discusses these matters is Francesco D'Ovidio, *Versificazione italiana e arte poetica medioevale* (Milan: Hoepli, 1910), 9-62.

37   J. G. F. Powell, "10. Hyperbaton and register in Cicero," *Colloquial and Literary Latin*, edited by Eleanor Dickey and Anna Chahoud, https://www.cambridge.org/core/books/abs/colloquial-and-literary-latin/hyperbaton-and-register-in-cicero/7BDC02B6FE229CB5735D76279B54494D, published online by Cambridge University Press: 04 April 2011.

38   "Elegiaco carmine, sono sue parole, amores luserat, quos quinque exaratos libris, religionis causa, ignibus tradidit; multa itidem rythmis lusit hetruscis, quæ pari causa par ignis absumpsit," *Johannes Franciscus Picus in Vita* cited by Father Felice Ceretti, *Sonetti Inediti del Conte Giovanni Pico della Mirandola Messi in Luce*, (Mirandola: 1894). Reprinted by Nabu Press, 2013, 7.

39   Ceretti, *Sonetti*, 10.

40   Ceretti, *Sonetti*, 11.

41   Francesco De Sanctis, *Storia della Letteratura Italiana*, v. 1, (Milano: Rizzoli, 1983), 426

42   Dilemmi, *Sonetti*, xi.

43 Armando Torno, "Viaggio all ricerca di Pico," in *Giovanni Pico della Mirandola, I Sonetti*, edited by Gabriella Sica, (Milano : La vita felice, 1996), 12.
44 My translations were facilitated by three main sources:

   1. With both text and erudite commentary serving as the basis for this translation, Giorgio Dilemmi, *Giovanni Pico della Mirandola Sonetti*, based on the Italian Codex 1543 in the Bibliothèque nationale de France.

   2. One of my dearest friends found several decades ago in the late 70s at Peter Keisogloff Rare & Fine Books in the Arcade in Cleveland, Ohio: Edgren, Hjalmar, assisted by Giuseppe Bico and John Lawrence Gerig, *An Italian and English Dictionary, With Pronunciation and Brief Etymologies* (New York: Henry Holt and Company, 1904)
      Edgren and his team based their dictionary in the main on Policarpo Petrocchi's *Novo Dizionario Scolastico della Lingua Italiana dell'uso e Fuori d'uso con la Pronunzia le Flessioni dei Nomi, le Contiugazioni e le Etimologie Secondo gli Ultimi Risultati della Moderna Linguistica*, 1899, and Petrocchi's *Dizionario universale della lingua italiana*, 1887. Edgren et al. also consulted Rigutini Fanfani's *Vocabolario italiano*, 1987; Francesco Zambaldi's *Vocabolario etimo logico italiano*, 1889; Giuseppe Baretti's *Dizionario italiano*, ed inglese, 1 & 2, 1790 and later dates; John Millhouse's *New English and Italian Pronouncing and Explanatory* Dictionary by John Millhouse, 1855 and William James and Giuseppe Grassi's *James-Grassi Dictionary of the Italian and English Languages* by William James and Giuseppe Grassi, 1887 later dates. Interesting to note that each of the aforementioned dictionairies are quickly available through the *Internet Archive*, which, on its own, is a pretty wonderful place.

   3. The online *Il Vocabolario del Trecanni*, the contemporary continuation of the classic 1927-1939 *Enciclopedia italiana*.

45 Croce writes of " ... the impossibility of translations, translations in so far as they pretend to effect the re-moulding of one expression into another, like a liquid poured from a vase of a certain shape into a vase of another shape ... we cannot reduce what has already possessed its aesthetic form to another form also aesthetic. Indeed, every translation either diminishes and spoils, or it creates a new expression, by putting the former back into the crucible and mingling it with the personal impressions of the so-called translator ... 'Faithful ugliness or faithless beauty' is a proverb that well expresses the dilemma with which every translator is faced. Benedetto Croce, *Aesthetic as Science of Expression and General Linguistic*, trans. Douglas Ainslie, (New York: Noonday Press, 1922), 68.

Printed in the USA
CPSIA information can be obtained
at www.ICGtesting.com
LVHW071233191024
794187LV00009B/133